Understanding and Managing Children's Beh through Group Work Ages 3–5

Understanding and Managing Children's Behaviour through Group Work Ages 3–5 provides the reader with an insight into children's emotional well-being and helps them to understand what and how children communicate and how to respond in a way that provides positive messages, increases their emotional vocabulary and encourages them to change their behaviour. It provides an alternative and effective child-centred way of managing children's behaviour through introducing the concept of reflective language and other tools, equipping staff with new skills that are transferable across the school in any role.

The book is divided into two sections, enabling the reader to link theory with practice. The first section takes the reader on a journey to help them understand the different factors that influence children's behaviour. The second section of the book focuses on the group work programmes: how they can be used; their value; and the impact they can have on children and the classroom environment as a whole. The activities in the group work programme explore the concept of using reflective language as a behaviour management tool and are designed to motivate and build confidence, self-esteem and resilience. Using pedagogical features throughout, the book includes:

- practitioner and classroom management tips and reflective tasks;
- strategies and practical ideas for staff to use to help them engage more deeply with the contents of the book;
- flexible, tried and tested group work programmes designed to promote inclusion rather than exclusion;
- clear, step by step instructions for delivering the work programmes;
- case studies showing behaviour examples with detailed explanations for the behaviour and strategies to respond to it.

The book is aimed at all early years practitioners and any students training to work with children of EYFS age. It is also recommended reading for SENCOs and trainee teachers, and will be useful for therapists who work with children and are looking at delivering other approaches in their work.

Cath Hunter is a therapeutic consultant and play therapist with over thirty years' experience of working with children, staff and families. Her academic experience includes lecturing on childcare and play work at City College Manchester, and working as a clinical supervisor at Liverpool Hope University, UK. www.therapeuticfamilyinterventions.co.uk

Understanding and Managing Children's Behaviour through Group Work Ages 3–5

A child-centred approach

Cath Hunter

Routledge
Taylor & Francis Group
LONDON AND NEW YORK

First published 2016
by Routledge
2 Park Square, Milton Park, Abingdon, Oxon OX14 4RN

and by Routledge
711 Third Avenue, New York, NY 10017

Routledge is an imprint of the Taylor & Francis Group, an informa business

British Library Cataloguing in Publication Data
A catalogue record for this book is available from the British Library

Library of Congress Cataloging in Publication Data
Names: Hunter, Cath.Title: Understanding and managing children's behaviour through group work ages 3-5 : a child-centred approach / Cath Hunter.Description: First published 2016. | New York : Routledge, 2016. | Includes bibliographical references.Identifiers: LCCN 2015042484| ISBN 9781138961074 (hardback) | ISBN 9781138961098 (pbk.) | ISBN 9781315660004 (ebook)Subjects: LCSH: Classroom management. | Problem children--Behavior modification. | Behavior disorders in children. | Education, Preschool.Classification: LCC LB3013 .H825 2016 | DDC 371.102/4--dc23LC record available at http://lccn.loc.gov/2015042484

ISBN: 978-1-138-96107-4 (hbk)
ISBN: 978-1-138-96109-8 (pbk)
ISBN: 978-1-315-66000-4 (ebk)

Typeset in Helvetica
by GreenGate Publishing Services, Tonbridge, Kent

Printed and bound by CPI Group (UK) Ltd, Croydon, CR0 4YY

Dedicated to Brenda and Jack

Contents

	List of figures and tables	viii
	Foreword by Carol Powell	ix
	Acknowledgements	xi
	Introduction	xii
	Part One: Theory	
	A child-centred approach to emotional health and well-being and understanding children's behaviour	1
1	What does a child need to be emotionally healthy?	3
2	The impact of external circumstances on a child's ability to learn and succeed at school	17
3	What is this child trying to tell me?	29
4	Integrating emotional well-being into the whole school	43
5	Developing positive and meaningful relationships at school	57
6	You can make a difference	71
	Part Two: Practice	
	Using group work to promote emotional health and well-being and manage children's behaviour	77
7	The benefits of group work	79
8	The role of the group facilitator	88
9	Starting and ending group work	91
10	'What ifs' for group work	97
11	Friendship programme and facilitator's guidelines	98
12	Self-esteem programme and facilitator's guidelines	111
	Conclusion	124
	Resources	125
	Resources for friendship group	133
	Resources for self-esteem group	142
	Index	147

List of figures and tables

Figures

2.1	Who am I?	28
3.1	The cycle of misunderstanding	36
3.2	Breaking the cycle of misunderstanding	38
7.1	Positive messages to children	84
8.1	Positive impact of reflecting	89
9.1	Potential negative impact of facilitator	94
9.2	Potential positive impact of facilitator	95

Tables

1.1	How group work promotes emotional health and well-being	15
2.1	Potential barriers to learning	17
2.2	Impact of parent behaviour on child	18
2.3	Developing a positive internal belief system	19
2.4	Conflicting messages between home and school	20
2.5	Expressing feelings in the family	23
2.6	Development of internal belief system	25
3.1	Understanding behaviour	30
3.2	Links between physical and emotional well-being	34
3.3	What is this behaviour telling us?	37
4.1	Potential emotional impact of the school day	43
4.2	Impact of positive reflective responses	50
4.3	Useful attributes	54
5.1	Development of core beliefs within the family	59
5.2	What has this child been taught in their family?	61
5.3	Impact of adult's response on child's behaviour	65
7.1	Impact of group work programme	80
7.2	Examples of experiences shared by children at the end of the session	83

Foreword

There is never an uneventful start of the day in our school, and on one particular Tuesday morning, Cath and I stood together watching Jack hurtle down the long and tempting expanse that is our bottom corridor. I shouted, 'Jack, walk!' Cath just laughed and said, 'Not yet, Carol.' And what was Jack's reaction? He was oblivious to us both and carried on as if released from a spinning top. Jack, at that time, had just started in Year 1. He was 5 years old and had recently started play therapy with Cath.

Sadly, Jack's story, though shocking, is not unusual: born addicted to heroin and never having connected with his birth mother, he lives with his older sister on a residency order. He looked and behaved like a much younger child and spent the school day in solitary but fairly physical activity. Trying to teach Jack was rather like trying to catch water! Enter Cath: her expert advice and calm manner gave Jack space to relax and to discover himself in the safe and undirected environment of the play room. Jack engaged with Cath immediately, though she reported that she needed extra time to tidy the play room after his sessions, and every time she walked him back to class he ran ahead of her and we all heard him coming!

Cath stuck with him, she gave advice to his teachers about how to teach him and spent time helping his sister learn about his needs, and gently directed her in ways of meeting those needs. When specialists knee-jerked into a diagnosis of ADHD for him, Cath helped me write a letter asking them to wait for the play therapy to work its magic before medicating him.

Jack is one of our individuals with severe difficulties; his life chances were compromised before he was born, but with Cath's support we are helping him to catch up. Cath has worked like this in our school and others to help children like Jack and those who are experiencing less severe but still significant challenges in life. She has worked with teachers to develop their skills and knowledge so that they can teach and interact with all children in a calm and effective manner. Her way of working and her sound advice are now accessible to many more teachers and their teams in this easy-to-follow and, ultimately, practical guide. Cath writes with authority and, as she does everything, with empathy. Her ideas are easy to implement and tried and tested – they work. She has worked in schools and knows the challenges facing many of us who are trying to provide well for children who have become out of kilter with their worlds. She writes so clearly because she has experienced these challenges first hand – her methods are underpinned with specialist knowledge about how children develop and what they need to flourish.

I cannot recommend Cath's book highly enough; its purpose is to help and support those of us who are trying to get it right – it comes from a compassionate place. This book will definitely be joining our staff library.

And what of Jack now? A year on, he walks down the corridor and sits with his peers on the carpet in his classroom. He stays still long enough to listen. He is learning and making progress, though he still struggles to grasp ideas that other children of his age manage to understand.

Perhaps the biggest indicator of Jack's development is that last week, as Cath and I stood in the corridor talking, he came up to her, hugged her and then, in complete charge of himself, walked up to his classroom. Now he has a chance.

Carol Powell
Head teacher

Acknowledgements

I would like to express my thanks and gratitude to the following people who have helped to make this book possible:

The head teachers who employ me and demonstrate their ongoing commitment to understanding, supporting and valuing the work I carry out in their schools.

Carol Powell, for her thoughtful contribution in writing the Foreword.

The school staff that have the courage and capacity to think about children in a different way and implement the strategies and techniques I suggest during staff consultations and training.

The teaching assistants, learning mentors and family workers in schools who have used these programmes, especially Kerry Edwards, Lauren Longsden and Hannah Hayhurst, for their ongoing dedication to implementing the programmes in their schools and having a significant impact on the children they have worked with. Their commitment to implementing reflective language across their roles in school has made a difference to many children.

Clare Farmer also deserves a special mention for her many years of dedication and commitment to children's emotional well-being.

Debbie Estkowski, my supervisor, for the many years of support and wisdom she has provided.

Sue Taplin, for her time, support and creative contribution to the Resources section.

My friends, for accepting seeing less of me and supporting me in a variety of different ways.

Jane O'Neill, because I really couldn't have done it without you.

Introduction

For many staff working in primary schools today, their desire to support and encourage learning is disrupted by children who do not conform to the expectations of engaged participation in daily school life. We may know of children who refuse to follow instructions, appear to be deliberately disruptive and challenge staff. We may also know of children who are withdrawn, overly eager to please and unable to build and sustain relationships. In some schools there may only be a few children causing concern, in others there may be many. This book is aimed at helping school staff to understand and support these children in achieving their full potential at school.

For children in our schools who are living with emotional instability and erratic and inconsistent parenting, this is a momentous task. There are also some children who have experienced trauma in their lives to varying degrees, which has a huge impact on their ability to feel safe and results in their experiencing high levels of stress and anxiety on a daily basis. For these children, their ability to settle at school and fully engage with their learning can be severely hampered by the external circumstances they are living in, making the job for school staff an enormous one of meeting emotional needs, managing behaviour and providing a stimulating learning environment.

The purpose of this book is to provide a greater insight into children's behaviour and enable school staff to increase their awareness of what children may be trying to communicate through their behaviour. It is aimed at encouraging different ways of thinking about children and facilitating a better understanding of their difficulties by encouraging school staff to explore the possible meanings behind children's actions. It will focus on increasing understanding of why a child may be doing something, rather than just looking at the behaviour the child is displaying. It also examines the importance of helping children with their feelings instead of just trying to get them to stop their behaviour. The book is divided into two parts to assist the reader to link the theory of supporting emotional health and well-being and improving behaviour with the practical tools to enable school staff to achieve this on a daily basis.

School staff can be confronted with children exhibiting challenging behaviour, which ensures they are visible and known to school staff on a regular basis. This book is aimed at exploring the possible reasons why children may be showing these behaviours, along with providing strategies that can be implemented in class to enable them to make positive changes. It is also aimed at raising awareness of children who may be less visible and require additional support to ensure they are noticed and their needs are met. It introduces accessible and successful techniques and strategies for school staff to use to improve children's self-esteem and relational behaviour, and promote emotional health and well-being.

I hope it will encourage staff to reflect on a child's behaviour and communications in order to improve understanding and promote a greater awareness of the impact of external circumstances on their mental health and well-being. This knowledge may then affect how adults respond to children, which may in turn positively influence the relationship between staff and children. When adults are open to making small changes in the way they view and respond to children's behaviour, this can have a positive impact on children, enabling them to feel more accepted and understood. The techniques and suggestions focus on strengthening the adult–child relationship and may also enable school staff to feel more competent and confident in their role in school.

As children spend a large proportion of their lives at school, they play a crucial role in providing a range of social experiences, as well as playing a key part in developing resilience in children. Schools play a vital part in both teaching and modelling relationships and life skills to children.

When children have difficult experiences outside school, they may not be well equipped to manage school and engage with their learning. The group work programmes focus on equipping children to develop skills such as patience and perseverance, along with the experience of compassion and empathy for others. These essential life skills may not be developed in the child's family but are essential for them to access the curriculum and achieve at school. Schools are in an ideal position to help them with this and provide them with the skills to have a successful life. This book examines the importance of considering children's individual needs and social and emotional needs, which are as important as a child's learning needs and have a huge impact on their ability to engage with their learning.

An awareness and understanding of children's emotional health and well-being is imperative for their general well-being and learning. Children's physical and emotional safety, needs and well-being need to come first and be a priority for schools in order for children to be happy, safe and secure and reach their full potential. In school we may ask children to perform tasks that may expose them or make them feel vulnerable, such as reading aloud in class or having a part in an assembly or school play. Children need to feel safe and secure in order to do this. When a child finds it difficult to put their feelings into words, they are at a disadvantage at school in terms of making and sustaining friendships and being able to access the curriculum. Children who are able to understand and express their feelings are able to achieve success at school and reach their potential more easily.

Using reflective language is a key concept of this book, and in my experience is one of the most powerful tools that can change children's behaviour and set them on the path to improved mental health and well-being. The reflective language used throughout the book, and particularly in the facilitator's notes that accompany each session, can be used with children in any context and provide a different approach to working with children. This unique and easy-to-use method helps to develop self-awareness, self-control and resilience, all of which are essential ingredients for emotional health and well-being. The staff who have delivered the group work programmes have reported the effectiveness of using this tool both in the sessions and in their other roles around the school as a way of managing behaviour. They have also noticed that their increased self-awareness has resulted in an improved understanding of children's behaviour. The concrete examples of reflective language and staff reflective practice provided in this book enable school staff to become more aware of what, why and how children communicate through their behaviour, along with increasing their awareness of how they respond to this. This change in staff thinking can result in a better understanding of themselves and why they react to certain situations, along with an increased awareness of other school staff. This improved working relationship may result in a positive impact on the children.

I invite all school staff, regardless of their role, to try the staff strategies and reflections, and explore using reflective language. This may be a new way of behaving for school staff: experiment with it, use it tentatively, using words such as 'wondering' or 'perhaps' or 'sometimes', rather than telling. While reading this book, I encourage you to think about the children you work with on a daily basis and consider what they may be trying to communicate to you through their behaviour. Throughout the book I use 'can' or 'may' to reiterate the importance of remembering that all children are individuals and therefore may respond differently to situations.

I will refer to my own experiences of delivering the group work programmes, along with the experiences of staff who have implemented them, as all of the group work activities have been delivered by me and teaching assistants, learning mentors and family workers. The staff delivering the group work felt it enhanced their understanding of children's behaviour and gave them an insight into what the children were trying to communicate. The other school staff, including head teachers, commented on the noticeable changes in the children after the intervention and felt that it helped them to be more integrated into school life. The group work is most effective when it is delivered as part of a whole school approach to emotional health and well-being.

The group work programmes in this book are tried and tested and have been successfully implemented by school staff in a variety of roles across several schools. They can be delivered easily throughout the school year and provide an ideal opportunity for more focused work for children who need extra support with their social and emotional development. The activities are devised as a six-week programme but can be adapted for use with individuals or pairs of children in a way that meets children's needs. The group work programmes provide an opportunity for children to practise and develop skills that increase the likelihood of them being socially included, rather than excluded from school and society as a whole.

In order to protect the confidentiality of the children and staff, any case studies or examples are composite and names and details have been changed. They are drawn from a number of experiences from my work over several years.

I hope you enjoy this book and the activities, and that it enables you to think differently about the children you work with.

Part One: Theory

A child-centred approach to emotional health and well-being and understanding children's behaviour

1 What does a child need to be emotionally healthy?

In order for children to achieve success at school they need a degree of healthy emotional and social development so that they are emotionally ready and able to learn. The key issues for children aged 3–5 years is their ability to separate easily from their parents and adjust to being at school, which is strongly affected by their attachment and the security of the relationship they have with them. They need to be able to deal with this separation in order to be able to manage the school day and all it entails. (I will discuss this further in Chapter 5.) Managing the school day includes having a sense of confidence, self-esteem, self-reliance and independence appropriate to their age, along with the ability to be able to manage change and unpredictability without its eroding their feelings of safety and security. They also need to have the social skills to develop, build and sustain relationships with both adults and children, and to be able to ask for help when they need it. How many children start school equipped with all the skills to be able to do this?

The experience of being emotionally healthy is achieved by a combination of all these skills together and not in isolation, in the same way as a child's ability to hold a pencil is dependent on their hand–eye coordination and manipulative skills. It is the cumulative effect of the child's experiences, learned behaviours and reactions to events that help define their sense of self and their ability to deal with situations both in and out of school. Children need information and explanations about what is happening in order for them to be able to make sense of their experiences.

A child's social and emotional development is a crucial foundation and provides them with a sense of themselves and enables them to establish quality relationships with other people. A strong social and emotional foundation will enable a child to connect with others, resolve conflicts, achieve success and experience happiness in life.

Self-regulation

In order for children to be able to regulate their own stress levels, they need to have had this experience from an adult. Babies are unable to regulate their own stress and they depend on their caregivers to regulate it for them. For example, when a baby cries because they are hungry, tired or upset and the adult responds with love and concern, this helps to reduce the baby's stress. If a crying baby is ignored or met with anxiety or hostility, it can increase their stress. The way the adult responds to this stress can either help the child to develop their own stress regulatory system, or create even more stress and prevent this development taking place. If the child gets what they need from an adult, then a pattern develops that allows the child to begin to manage stress for themselves.

Depending on a child's experiences, by the age of three they may be beginning to understand some of the feelings they are experiencing, but are unlikely to have developed much impulse control. Therefore, if they want something they will often take action to get it, such as snatching from other children. The concept of delayed gratification is a particularly difficult one for children of this age to understand; they want things immediately and may express strong reactions, such as raging tantrums, when being asked to wait for things. It is a natural stage of children's development that they are egocentric up to about the age of four, depending on their experiences, and therefore it is very hard for them to see anything from another person's perspective, i.e. 'Why would I want to give someone else a sweet when I can keep it for myself?' They may find it hard to understand why they can't have what they want when they want it and become stressed and agitated, making this behaviour particularly hard to manage in school, where there may be several children who behave in this way. It can be useful and help children's emotional development if adults respond to children's stress in a way that calms and soothes them rather than in a way that exacerbates their stress.

For example, Tom, aged 3, is happily playing with a train when another child snatches it from him. Tom screams with rage and hits the child. If he is soothed, comforted, listened to and supported, then this validates his feelings and enables stress regulatory systems to be developed. If he is offered a calm and clear explanation about not hitting other children, then he is gradually able to understand that this behaviour is not acceptable. Tom is totally dependent on the stress regulating systems of a caring adult to help him to develop his own. If a caring adult is able to help him with his feelings and acknowledge and soothe his distress, he gradually develops the ability to do this for himself. As stressful situations occur in his life, he has the ability to manage them due to his initial experiences of stress being held and helped by a caring adult. When a child's parent or carer is able to regulate their own feelings and demonstrate positive and healthy ways of managing their own stress and anxiety, this is beneficial to the child who has this as a template of how to deal with feelings.

However, if the adult responds to the situation by shouting at him, dragging him away or smacking him for hitting the other child, Tom will feel even more stressed and anxious and will be unable to develop self-regulation. He does not learn how to manage stress and anxiety for himself; instead he learns to be wary and fearful of other people and finds it extremely difficult to share. He is overwhelmed by his feelings and unable to self-regulate. He may learn that feelings are to be feared and avoided at all times, rather than managed and expressed in a healthy way.

Case study

Jake, aged 4, had regular tantrums at school. He would snatch things from other children, refuse to share things and got very upset and angry if he didn't get his own way. He would shout and cry and become very agitated.

Possible reasons for Jake's behaviour:

- His parents worked long hours and felt guilty about not spending time with him, so they overindulged him and found it very hard to say 'no' to him.
- His older brother regularly had tantrums, which resulted in him getting his own way.

This resulted in Jake trying to achieve the same result at school as he got at home, and becoming very confused and upset when this did not happen. When children have not had the experience of self-regulation being provided by a parent, school staff can contribute to helping them with this and fulfilling this role.

Strategies to help children to self-regulate

- Respond to the intensity of what the child is feeling and reinforce this with an affirming tone of voice and facial expression; for example, 'It made you furious that you couldn't be at the front of the line today.'
- Validate the child's experience; it is very real for them, so ensure they feel you are taking it seriously; for example, 'When Sam called you stupid, it must have really hurt.'
- Support the child by helping them to find alternative ways to express their feelings, if appropriate; for example, 'It's never okay to hit people, Michael. We need to find other ways that you can have your feelings and not hurt anyone when you have them.'
- Provide a calm and reassuring approach, so the child feels you are affirming them and accepting rather than dismissing their feelings; for example, 'It can be really difficult when you want to have the red pen and someone else is already using it.'
- Use regular opportunities during the school day to comment on children's non-verbal signs of emotion; for example, 'I can see you look a bit cross about having to wait your turn'.

The above responses enable the child to feel connected to, understood and recognised for who they are and what they are feeling. It gives the message 'all feelings are okay and I can help you with them'. It helps them to make the link between feelings and words, which is crucial for children, as they can experience their emotions intensely and need help, support and the emotional vocabulary to make sense of what is happening. It affirms the pain the child is feeling and helps them to understand it. This helps them to feel less overwhelmed and alone with the feelings and therefore less scared. This will support the child with developing self-regulation. When an adult intervenes and offers support, it can reduce the anxiety levels for children as well as validate, rather than invalidate, their experiences and feelings.

Staff strategy – helping children to self-regulate

Provide activities that are soothing and calming, such as sorting buttons or counters to help children to regulate their feelings.

Children need constant reminders of the behaviour that adults would like to see and explanations of what is expected of them and why. Children require boundaries that can be understood, and therefore it is useful to check their understanding of the rules and expectations that are in place at school and ensure these are clear and realistic to enable all children to experience success. For example, demonstrating how to tidy up rather than assuming all children have the experience of doing this at home. The use of visual reminders can also be a useful way of keeping a connection with a child and enabling them to practise regulating their behaviour.

Staff strategy – visual reminder

Take photos of the child doing the behaviour you would like to see; for example, sitting on the carpet. Show the child the picture of this at the relevant time and frequently throughout the day to help them understand what they need to do.

The role of the facilitator in the group work programmes enables the children in the group to practise self-regulation and provides an opportunity for the facilitator to transfer these new skills to their role across the school. This alternative way of responding to children's feelings and behaviour can be modelled across the school and empowers all staff to use a different approach.

Staff strategy – releasing feelings

If a child needs help to manage their feelings of anger and frustration, offer them a large scribble pad and pens or crayons for them to use when they need to. Ensure they are able to access them easily and offer support and demonstrations, if needed. Explain to the child that this can help them when they feel angry.

This activity provides a powerful message that all feelings are acceptable and an alternative and constructive way of helping a child to release them. It can be a useful tool to assist them in the process of self-regulation.

Developing independence

School life and all it entails requires children to have some level of autonomy and to become increasingly independent as they progress through school. The experience of becoming more independent and developing a sense of self is crucial, and an important developmental task for children aged 3–5 years is the ability to separate easily from their parent and manage without them for the school day. This can sometimes be difficult and can cause a great deal of distress, especially if they have not often been separated before. It can be particularly hard for children who have not experienced consistent and predictable parenting, as they may be even more anxious about if and when their parent will return for them at the end of the day. Starting school for the first time, coupled with leaving their parent or carer, can be a challenge for even the most secure child. The process of separation and independence is a gradual one that school can help with by finding the right balance between nurturing, protecting and guiding children and allowing them to explore and experiment. This enables them to develop some self-sufficiency and security in themselves and is assisted by having a caring adult in school who can be in tune with and responsive to their needs.

A child's ability to develop self-reliance and do things independently depends on several factors and is affected by their confidence and self-esteem, along with the opportunity to develop these skills. In school there may be an expectation that children have a level of independence that enables them to cope with the school activities. For a child who has no experience of this at home, perhaps because they are treated like a baby to meet their parent's needs to feel wanted, the very experience of this can be daunting.

Case study

Chloe, aged 4, was often late for school, and her mum would undo her coat and hang it up on her peg for her. She would then choose a pen and try it to see if it worked before giving it to Chloe to write her name on her whiteboard, as she did every morning at the start of the school day. Chloe was often standing around sucking her fingers and waiting to be directed to activities. She was frequently upset at leaving her mum and found it hard to settle after the weekend or a school holiday.

Possible reasons for Chloe's behaviour:

- Chloe's dad died when she was one and her mum was very protective of her.
- When Chloe tried to do things for herself, she was discouraged and her mum took over, insisting she was only a baby.

It can be both frustrating and challenging for school staff having a child like Chloe in school, but it also provides an ideal opportunity for her to experience support for the essential aspects of her development she has missed out on. It provides a very useful opportunity to work with her mum on encouraging Chloe to be more independent, especially if the school employs a family worker who can provide some additional support to parents who have experienced difficulties that may impact on their child being able to settle and reach their full potential at school.

Strategies to promote independence

- Offer opportunities for children to make choices on a regular basis to develop confidence in their own abilities.
- Identify children who need additional help with self-care skills and provide opportunities for this throughout the day.
- Create special jobs for children to build confidence and develop new skills.
- Name the possible feelings that the child may be experiencing, e.g. 'I can see you're looking unsure; I am wondering if it's very difficult for you to put your shoes on.'

When children experience being independent and developing new skills as a positive event that involves them having more freedom, this encourages them to persevere with tasks and situations they may otherwise have found difficult or frustrating. This results in an increased sense of themselves as strong and capable, rather than helpless and inadequate. This increases the likelihood of children becoming more independent, resulting in increased confidence, self-esteem and self-belief.

Self-reliance

Case study

Leon, aged 4, was very independent and found it very hard to ask for help. At school he would struggle to put his coat on and do the zip up by himself, turning away from any offers of help from school staff and insisting he could do it.

Possible reasons for Leon's behaviour:

- He was the oldest of three children and often helped with his younger siblings.
- He frequently looked after his mum, who was a single parent and had periods of depression and was often very quiet and absorbed in her own thoughts.

It was impossible for him to ask for or allow himself to receive help, as he'd learned to rely on the only person that had always been there for him: himself. He had learned to adopt self-reliance as a way of coping and feared neediness or asking for help as it had not been available for him. At school he presented as someone who was self-contained and could manage on his own.

This resulted in him finding relationships with both children and adults challenging, as he was controlling and manipulative as a way of feeling safe in his world.

In order for children to develop a sense of independence and ability to depend on themselves, it helps if they have had an experience of being able to depend on an adult who has responded appropriately to their needs. For a child who has not had this experience, or it has been inconsistent, it can feel terrifying to both ask for help and be able to receive it. These children have learned to be overly reliant on themselves as a way of feeling safe and will need plenty of support to change this behaviour. They may think, 'I can only rely on myself'. The challenge for these children is to trust that an adult will consistently support them and to understand that it is acceptable to ask for help from others.

Strategies for children who are overly reliant on themselves

- Understand that they have learned to do this as a way of feeling safe and ensure you do not take over or invade their space; for example, provide opportunities for them to play near you so they can access you easily and you can monitor them if they need help.
- Identify their need to do things for themselves and reflect on what it may feel like to change this; for example, 'I can see you are struggling to do that on your own; I wonder what it would feel like if I helped you with it?'
- Let them lead their relationship with you and gradually access help in their own time and at their own pace by gentle reminders that you are available and willing to help them; for example, 'You are working very hard doing that puzzle; remember I can help you at any time if you need it.'
- Provide strong messages that validate it is okay to ask for help and model this with the other members of staff; for example, 'Mrs Jacobs, please could you help me carry that box; everyone needs help with things sometimes, and it's okay to ask other people to help us.'

The experience of developing self-reliance and becoming more independent is a gradual process that develops throughout childhood. In order for a child to achieve this in a healthy way, it is necessary to provide them with opportunities to experience this. It can sometimes be a challenge for school staff to find the balance between encouraging independence and dependence when working with children of this age.

Strategies to help children develop self-reliance

- Provide regular opportunities during the day for children to carry out tasks for themselves; for example, getting their own bag and coat at the end of each day.
- Identify opportunities to help other children with small tasks; for example, 'Please could you help Chloe tidy the book corner?'
- Ensure that children are rewarded for their efforts as well as their achievements; for example, 'You tried very hard to find your hat. Well done!'
- Talk to the child's parents and identify something they have done well or achieved that day and encourage them to see the importance of the child having opportunities to do things for themselves at home.

Self-confidence and self-esteem

A child's sense of self-worth is deeply affected by their confidence and self-esteem. For children who have a poor sense of self, the school day can be made up of regular experiences that can erode this even further. It is useful for school staff to consider where a child is in terms of their social and emotional development; for example, are they developmentally four or are they still at the toddler age of being unable to share and take turns? If this is the case, they need opportunities to practise and develop these skills during the school day with a sensitive and patient adult. It is important that children's social and emotional developmental levels are assessed to ascertain the additional support they may need, in the same way as their literacy and numeracy levels may be, so the appropriate help can be provided.

Children develop self-esteem from feeling capable and being able to demonstrate new skills, so it is essential to provide regular opportunities for them to experience this. A child with confidence and self-esteem is keen to try new things and has the ability to develop and maintain good relationships with adults and children alike. They are able to express feelings such as excitement and fear with equal confidence. They have learned to trust the adults in their lives to care for and support them and therefore have the ability do this for other people. They may believe they are essentially good and likeable and experience other people as the same. There are also frequent opportunities throughout the school day to enhance this and ensure that it is developed to maximise the child's full potential.

However, some children's experiences have resulted in them having a very different sense of themselves. They experience the world as a frightening and unsafe place, where it is better not to try new things in case you fail or make a mistake. They have discovered that some adults are unpredictable and that things change frequently and therefore nothing can be relied on. They have learned that feelings are to be feared and kept to yourself, as they can overwhelm you and make things even more frightening. A child with low self-esteem may present as being unsure of themselves at school. They may resist or find excuses not to try new things and may find it hard to express and manage their feelings. They may believe they are essentially bad and unlikeable and experience other people as better than them and more deserving.

Staff strategy – achievement awards

Create achievement awards to present to children for being kind, helpful, etc. Present the award to a child before going home each day, ensuring each child has a chance to receive one at some point during the term. For example, Kashif has been .... today (insert word such as 'helpful').

Strategies to develop confidence and self-esteem

- Provide opportunities to make choices wherever possible throughout the day, no matter how small; for example, choosing where to sit at times during the day so they feel they have a voice and their opinions are important.
- Identify positive aspects of who they are and how they behave; for example, 'You were really kind when you picked the pencil up off the floor.'
- Acknowledge and praise them for their achievements and successes, no matter how small.
- Introduce emotional vocabulary to them; for example, 'It can make us feel scared when we hear a loud noise.'

It is essential to give children the opportunity to make choices, no matter how small, as it gives them positive messages about themselves. It enables them to be assertive and state their wishes in an acceptable way and conveys that they can be trusted to make their own decisions, even if they are different from the ones an adult may choose for them. The experience of feeling that you can be trusted to make your own decisions has a big impact on a child's self-belief and sense of feeling valued and worthwhile, so it is crucial that schools provide as many opportunities for this as possible throughout the school day. It also enables them to have first-hand experience of learning about choices and consequences, which is essential for emotional well-being.

Children who appear over confident

There may also be children in school who appear to be over confident and demand that they be chosen for everything, appear to know all the answers and may present as being happy in themselves. However, this may be a result of needing to be in control and manage situations around them in order to feel safe. This behaviour may be observed in children who have experienced domestic violence or other traumatic experiences and are desperately trying to establish some sense of security and stability in their lives. They may behave in ways that are challenging to school staff, such as questioning them and saying they don't want to do things. This may be caused by their need to test adults in order to ascertain their reactions to events; for example, 'Miss Brogan always seems very happy, but I am sure I can make her sad if I hit someone.' This may not be a calculated and conscious process, but can be a coping mechanism the child has learned in order to get a response from adults.

This child may have also learned to feel over responsible for the adults in their life and need to check out whether all adults are unpredictable. While this behaviour can be challenging to deal with at times, it can be useful to explore what may be going on for the child and how they may be feeling. It can be difficult for school staff to accept that children who present as controlling and challenging may actually be feeling frightened and vulnerable. However, if children feel that school staff are unable to manage them, they may feel scared, and this can reaffirm the negative feelings they already have about themselves.

Strategies for children who appear over confident

- Remain in charge and be predictable wherever possible, so they feel safe and secure.
- Prepare them in advance for any changes that may occur, in order to develop their ability to trust that adults mean what they say.
- Acknowledge and express emotional reactions to things; for example, 'Being in a different room can make us feel worried, as we are not used to it.' This may encourage them to begin to voice their own feelings in situations where they feel uncomfortable.

Self-image

Children who have a positive self-image are able to share their happiness about their appearance in a healthy way; for example, showing you their new shoes or haircut. This is an important aspect of children learning to be happy with who they are and, along with self-confidence and self-esteem, plays a role in self-acceptance. A child who has a poor self-image may put themselves down by criticising their appearance and making comments such as, 'I don't like my hair'. This may demonstrate a deeper sense of self-loathing and needs to be monitored closely. These children may be particularly vulnerable to being bullied by other children, especially as they start to become more aware of appearances as they get older. A balance between the two extremes is emotionally healthy, where a child is happy to get themselves and their clothes dirty playing outside, but is also happy to wash their hands when they return to class.

Strategies to promote a positive self-image

- Monitor children who avoid messy activities and don't like getting dirty, and encourage them to participate by providing aprons and acknowledging their anxieties; for example, 'You seem unsure about getting paint on your hands; remember, we can wash them afterwards.'
- Share positive comments about children's appearance where relevant and appropriate, without embarrassing them or excluding other children.

Self-belief

Children who have a strong self-belief are able to share their thoughts and ideas and have a sense of determination that motivates them to do well. They are able to commit to achieving their goals and work towards them; for example, finishing making something. This self-belief is initially developed through external mechanisms such as parental support and encouragement and rewards. This is particularly important for children in early primary, who are reliant on the feedback from adults for their sense of self-worth and thrive on praise, acceptance and validation and have often not yet developed an internal sense of self-validation. They also may not have a solid enough sense of who they are to be able to cope with criticism or failure and can find this very difficult to manage without plenty of adult support and reassurance.

Schools can play a crucial role in supporting children who have little or no self-belief, and while this is initially a slow process, it is one that is achievable and can make a fundamental difference to children's lives. The development of self-belief initially starts within the family, and for a child who lives with criticism, hostility and rejection, it is an enormous task to alter what they have learned and experienced. A child's sense of self-worth can be activated by instilling a sense of them deserving to experience good things in their life. This is difficult but crucial for children who have experienced rejection or who have a sense of themselves as not being good enough. The work of school staff in managing this is immense but achievable.

Strategies to develop self-belief

- Identify attributes you appreciate in children and share these with them; for example, 'I can see you were being really kind when you were helping Matthew find his shoes.'
- Acknowledge children's efforts and attempts at achieving things; for example, 'You tried hard to share today; well done for trying.'
- Introduce motivational vocabulary throughout the day; for example, 'I could see you worked really hard when you were doing the jigsaw today.'

Personal responsibility and self-awareness

An understanding of personal responsibility and self-awareness is necessary for a child to be able to change their behaviour. The combination of both of these enables a child to understand about important concepts such as differences of opinion and acceptance of other people. The ability to accept themselves and their own strengths and areas to work on enables children to develop this same acceptance of other people. This is linked closely with self-regulation, confidence and self-belief, as they are all necessary ingredients for self-awareness and personal responsibility. This concept can be difficult for some children to understand. In some families, difference may be seen as something negative, and this provides an alternative way to view this.

Self-awareness is crucial to the development of self-control. If children have an understanding of personal responsibility, they are able to acknowledge when they make mistakes and accept accountability for the choices they have made. They have a strong enough sense of themselves to be able to accept that getting things wrong is an important part of learning and to move on from this. They are aware that their behaviour has an impact on other people and are able to recognise when it may be appropriate to change this for other people's benefit. For a child to manage consequences, they need to be able to manage the feelings that may arise from doing something wrong. For example, Josh, aged 4, punches another child who tries to take the ball he is playing with. In order for Josh to accept the consequences of his behaviour, he needs to be able to experience the feelings of sadness, upset, anger and frustration that may arise from the consequence he has been given. However, he also needs to be able to separate his behaviour from his sense of self, i.e. 'I did something wrong, but I am still a good person.' For some children, this is where the difficulty lies and why their behaviour may deteriorate into a spiral of negative behaviour after one incident.

For these children, it can be difficult for them to hold on to a positive sense of themselves when they interpret that they are being told the opposite, i.e. 'I hurt someone, therefore I am a bad person.' They need help and support to tolerate and make sense of the difficult feelings they are experiencing, and this can be helped by an adult acknowledging and exploring some of the possible feelings with them. For example, 'It can make us feel really angry when someone takes something we are playing with; I could see you were playing nicely before that happened.' This recognition and acceptance of the child's feelings and experience may enable the child to maintain a more positive view of himself both during and after the experience, along with enabling him to accept his consequence more easily.

The concepts of patience, being kind and honest can be difficult to understand and implement if this is not your experience outside school. When children have had little or no evidence of this experience operating within their family, it may be very difficult for them to grasp. It is important that we spend time explaining these ideas and their meaning to children, rather than assume they already have an understanding. It is crucial that we demonstrate the behavioural expectations we have of children in school in order to maximise their chances of integrating them. For example, the concept of being kind may be a difficult one for children to understand, and it can be helpful to give them examples of this on a daily basis, such as identifying and naming specific situations when this occurs during the school day. The concept of honesty can be hard for children to understand, especially if the adults in their family blame each other and other people when things go wrong or deny anything is their fault as 'things just happen'. Then it can be very confusing for children to understand the idea of actions having consequences and people having responsibility for the choices they make. It can also make it difficult for them to admit when they have done something or been dishonest.

The role of schools in providing opportunities for children to understand and gain positive experiences from these ideas is therefore crucial. The whole school ethos can be based around this and linked in to the behaviour and reward system. This is explored in more detail in Chapter 4.

Strategies to develop personal responsibility and self-awareness

- Discuss and celebrate uniqueness and differences between the children and staff in school so children value this as a positive experience.
- Provide opportunities to explore being kind so children understand these concepts; for example, 'Let's see how many times we can be kind today in class; I want you to help me find examples of when we are doing this.'
- Identify and praise children for their individual choices, especially if they are different from the other children's; for example, 'I see you're the only one to have used the green paper, Jamie. Well done for making the choice that you wanted.'

Resilience

The development of resilience can be viewed as one of the most vital ingredients for emotional health and well-being. The ability to deal with situations and bounce back after adversity is of paramount importance for all children, but especially those who live with uncertainty and disruption outside school. For children whose lives consist of them being criticised and ridiculed, or who live with drama and chaos, a sense of resilience is necessary for them to cope with this experience. The capacity for anyone to develop and sustain this is supported by the impact of other people who are able to encourage and believe in them, and therefore school staff play a crucial role in enabling children to feel competent.

In order to develop resilience, children need to experience some frustration to enable them to strengthen their ability to problem solve and learn. They need to be able to manage feelings of disappointment, failure and losing, which can be hard at any age, but is especially difficult for children aged 3–5. This process can be helped by school staff naming and acknowledging the potential feelings that can be activated in situations. For example, 'It can be really hard when we don't get chosen to do things; it may make us feel cross or sad.' While children may not always be able to tolerate frustration, the opportunity to experience this while being supported by a trusting adult is vital. School staff can support this experience by ensuring they resist the urge to over-help children.

The ability to practise having courage and facing fears can also contribute enormously to the development of resilience. A child who has experienced being brave and has had their experience validated by a caring adult is more able to strengthen these skills. Children who are resilient are able to develop strategies to support themselves when they experience difficult situations and therefore have their own bank of resources to use when life becomes challenging. Their experience of using a strategy that has worked enables them to use this again when they need to.

Strategies to develop resilience

- Provide opportunities for open and honest discussions about how we may feel and how to manage different situations; for example, falling out with friends, doing new things, etc.
- Introduce emotional vocabulary such as 'scared', 'worried', 'cross', 'angry' to enable children to understand and express what they and other people may be feeling
- Acknowledge situations where a child has faced their own challenge and discuss it with them, exploring the skills they feel they used; for example, 'You were very brave when you came and told me when Ryan was calling you names.'

It is essential that we consider how we can not only develop the resilience necessary for emotional health, but also have awareness of ensuring we do not destroy it. When a child's sense of self is fragile and gradually being developed by positive affirmations of who they are and what they do, we need to be aware of how easy it can be for this to disintegrate by comments, looks, tone of voice such as shouting, etc. While it is unrealistic and unhealthy to expect children to never be exposed to this, it is useful for school staff to develop a heightened awareness of this and to reflect on how their behaviour may be received by children. This is explored in more detail in Chapters 2 and 5.

For children to manage school life and all the highs and lows that come with it, they need to feel safe in themselves and safe in their world. School provides them with the opportunity to take risks, manage frustration, anxiety and disappointment, all of which are terrifying experiences for children who have little or no resilience and no positive experiences of this.

Inconsistencies

The experience of erratic and inconsistent parenting where children are provided with extremely rigid rules or no rules at all can make life very frightening and unsafe. For these children, the ability to control what they are able to in school by being manipulative and controlling of other people, including adults, is a strategy they have developed to make themselves feel safe in an ever-changing and unpredictable world. For a child who goes home on Monday with paint on his jumper and Mum reacts by laughing, then on Tuesday Mum reacts by screaming, this may internalise the message 'no matter what I do, I can't get it right'. For these children life can be very confusing and may feel full of despair and lacking in hope. This can result in them having extreme reactions to situations, such as sobbing and being distraught about a broken pencil. They may have no sense of responsibility and blame other people all the time. Their core belief about themselves may be, 'I'm a bad person; I don't deserve to be liked or happy.' They lack confidence, have low self-esteem and poor social skills, and may see themselves as worthless and have intense feelings of shame. They may refuse to participate as they feel, 'What's the point?' and can come across as defiant, aggressive or lazy at school. A stable relationship with a member of school staff may enable them to feel safe, supported and secure, as can a stimulating, structured and consistent routine.

In families where children are given too much or too little responsibility, they are either never able to be a child or never able to grow up. Children who are given too much responsibility, perhaps by being expected to care for younger siblings, can present as overly responsible and bossy in school. They may also present as always being passive and behaving in a way that demonstrates that their needs aren't important; for example, letting other children go first all the time or not telling an adult when they have been hurt. The children who are over protected and never given any responsibility may find it difficult to make choices, as they may have little or no sense of who they are and what they like and dislike. Having either an over- or under-protective parent can be damaging to a child's sense of self and their self-esteem, along with their sense of feeling safe and secure. Children who experience intensely critical parenting by them insisting on perfection, teasing, ridiculing, humiliating the child or shaming or discounting them by name-calling or ignoring them, may expect other adults in their lives to respond in the same way. At school these children may be constantly looking for evidence to affirm this negative sense of themselves as worthless.

Differences between home and school

In families where the acceptable way of communicating may be through anger and/or aggression, the social norms and expectations of school are very difficult for children to understand and follow. Children who live in constant fear and turmoil may find it difficult to relax and enjoy school, as they are constantly on the lookout for potential danger from other children, adults or the environment, whether these are real or imagined. This constant state of hyper vigilance is very stressful and children in these situations may have learned that it is not safe to relax, as they need to be constantly alert for danger. This has a detrimental effect on their attention and concentration, as well as impairing their social and emotional development.

If children grow up in families where there is often an abundance of drama and lots of stress and excitement around it, they may bring that experience into school and always be in the middle of every situation, telling long, dramatic and sometimes difficult-to-follow accounts of other people's behaviour. They may display lots of 'notice me' behaviours, such as calling out, sighing, saying they are hurt or unwell and playing the role of victim and 'poor me' extremely well. For these children, it is very difficult to manage the day-to-day life of school without the adrenalin rush of drama and excitement that they are used to, and they may seek to create it for themselves.

The written and unwritten codes of behaviour expected in school can be opposite to the expectations outside school for some children, resulting in confusion and poor conscience development. For children to feel safe, stable and secure, it helps if they have had an experience of this, along with a safe and consistent relationship with an adult. For some children, inconsistency and unpredictability are the norm and are familiar to them. They may have experienced parents who, although they are physically present, are emotionally absent and preoccupied with their own needs and therefore unaware of the needs of their child. These children can find school life extremely challenging, where they are unable to hide in the shadows and are brought into the spotlight by their behaviour.

Providing new experiences

In order to change these children's destructive views of themselves, they need plenty of new experiences where the adults are able to affirm their efforts at tasks, even if they don't succeed at or complete them, and to be provided with meaningful praise and encouragement. They may be preoccupied with the adult relationships at school and may struggle to focus on tasks and hear instructions. The group work programmes provide the opportunity of being in a small group with a familiar and consistent adult, at the same time and in the same place each week. This experience provides children with an opportunity to experience consistency and predictability. The emotional focus of the group provides children with the opportunity to have their feelings acknowledged and validated, rather than ignored or dismissed. If children are not able to express their feelings when they occur, the experience may stay in their body, resulting in them feeling stressed, anxious and scared. Children need experiences of being able to understand and share their feelings or they can be overwhelmed by them and feel lonely and frightened. The opportunity to practise expressing feelings within the group work sessions increases their ability to continue this outside the sessions.

The group work programmes have been designed to develop children's emotional health and well-being, along with providing them with essential skills for everyday life. The facilitator's guidelines to accompany each session focus on identifying, acknowledging and reflecting possible feelings, along with recognising possible difficulties, and praising and encouraging the children for their contributions. This approach enables the children to make links between their feelings and behaviour and experiment with different behaviours in a safe and supportive environment.

Table 1.1 How group work promotes emotional health and well-being

Experience in the group	Potential impact on the child
Children are praised and encouraged	Builds self-esteem
Opportunities to practise and develop new skills	Develops independence and self-reliance
Encourages children to work together	Develops social skills
Focuses on respecting and exploring differences	Teaches acceptance of self and others
Identifies and acknowledges feelings	Increases emotional vocabulary
Provides permission to get things wrong and make mistakes	Promotes self-acceptance and builds resilience
Identifies and acknowledges effort	Develops a sense of trust
Encourages a commitment to completing tasks	Promotes personal and group responsibility
Encourages children to take risks	Develops self-belief

Children who are emotionally healthy have the skills and ability to tolerate frustration and uncertainty and have a strong sense of themselves as valuable individuals. They are able to relate to others with the skills and confidence to build and develop positive relationships, and have the ability to treat themselves and others with value and respect. They have the skills and resilience to cope with life's disappointments and are able to appreciate and enjoy their own and other people's successes. The group work programmes provide an opportunity for children to practise and develop these skills, which are then transferable outside the group sessions into the rest of their school life, making the effects of the sessions long lasting.

2 The impact of external circumstances on a child's ability to learn and succeed at school

By the time children start school they have already received strong messages about themselves, other people and the world. They form their initial sense of themselves and how they are perceived as people from within the family, and this can be either positive or negative. A child's internal rule book is developed early, along with their template of how to build and manage relationships. The family models ways of managing feelings that provide children with experiences that they bring to school and use in their daily life. All of this occurs within the family, which can be seen as the child's first classroom. The more information that school staff are provided with about a child's background and experiences (while maintaining any necessary confidentiality issues), the better equipped they are to respond to the child's needs.

In Chapter 1 I discussed children needing familiarity, consistency and predictability in order to help them feel safe and secure. How many children experience this outside school? If children do not feel safe and secure, this impacts on their social and emotional development as well as their ability to settle and engage with their learning at school. They may find it harder to connect with and build relationships with other children and adults, and their preoccupation with fear and anxiety can affect their ability to try things and practise and develop new skills.

Physical well-being

There are some children who have many barriers that can prevent them accessing their learning and reaching their potential. If a child's basic needs for food, appropriate clothing and sufficient sleep are not being met, they are disadvantaged before they have entered the school building to start their day.

Table 2.1 Potential barriers to learning

Situation	Child is preoccupied with	Impacts on learning
Wearing sandals in winter	Feeling cold	Can't concentrate, shivers, rubs feet
Falling asleep on sofa very late at night	Feeling tired	Yawns, can't engage or retain information, poor concentration, lack of coordination, listless, lethargic, fidgety, no resilience, gets upset easily
Missing breakfast and other meals	Feeling hungry, thinking about lunchtime and food	Anxious about the time, and obsessed with food

Do my needs matter?

All human beings have basic emotional needs for love, validation, acknowledgement and understanding. Within the family a child receives messages about the importance of their needs, and accumulates experiences of how these are responded to. If their needs are responded to consistently by a loving, caring adult who tries to meet them on a regular basis, the child internalises a strong and positive sense of themselves as a worthwhile person whose needs are important and do matter. However, if a child is frequently ignored or met with hostility and resistance when they express their needs, they learn that they are not important or worthwhile and their needs do not matter. A child with this experience may conclude that other people's needs are more important than theirs and will put other people first and try and meet their needs; for example, a child in school who brings their own ball in and gives it to the other children in her class to play with, without playing with it themselves. If children receive messages such as 'don't want, don't need, don't expect, don't say much', it is extremely difficult for them to have a positive sense of themselves as a worthwhile person.

Table 2.2 Impact of parent behaviour on child

Parent behaviour	Child learns
Mum is always busy	I must not disturb her
Dad is often out with his friends and doesn't spend time with me	I am not interesting. Dad doesn't like me
Mum frequently shouts and is angry	I must not ask for things or make a fuss
Dad is always bad tempered and unhappy	I must be cheerful and try to make Dad happy
Both parents ignore the child	I am not important or worthwhile
Mum criticises the child on a regular basis	I am a bad person and unlovable

Children who live with these experiences constantly occurring can develop coping strategies as a way of surviving in the world. These may manifest in school by them being controlling, bossy and manipulative, as well as trying to please other people. When a child is controlling and challenges adults on a regular basis, they may present as having no fear and not being bothered, but they have developed this behaviour as a way of feeling safe in a world that often feels very unsafe. They may use this coping strategy as a way of managing their feelings; for example, 'If I pretend I don't care, then I won't feel hurt or upset.'

Case study

Zara, aged 5, found carpet time very difficult. She was very restless, always calling out, and would try and turn her teacher's face towards her when she was sitting near her.

Possible reasons for Zara's behaviour:

- Zara's mum was often on her mobile phone when she came to collect her from school.
- In the mornings at school her mum would be texting as Zara was trying to show her something in the class.

Zara had learned that she needs to literally make sure that her teacher sees her and has developed coping strategies to ensure this happens. Her teacher gave Zara a carpet mat to help her sit in the same place and to enable her to feel that she had something special that was just for her. Her teacher gave her the responsibility of getting it each day, after showing her how to sit on it and keep her arms and legs on the mat. She also gave her plenty of praise and encouragement for doing this.

The positive attention she was receiving from her teacher on a daily basis had enabled her to feel noticed and special and she no longer needed to create her own way of getting these needs met.

It's all my fault

Some children may experience themselves as undeserving and may feel overly responsible for things. This may be due to them operating socially and emotionally at a much younger level of development than their chronological age. They may learn that no matter what they do or how they do it, they are wrong. This can result in them internalising the belief that everything is their fault and they are wrong because they are a bad person. When children hear constant criticism from the adults in their lives, they absorb it and believe it to be true, resulting in them developing their own internal critical voice. If children grow up with frequent experiences of being criticised and blamed, they may believe that this is the norm. Consequently, they may have thoughts such as:

- 'I am so bad, I make Mum angry all the time.'
- 'I gave my teacher a sore throat because he shouted at me yesterday.'
- 'If I had eaten all of my dinner, Dad wouldn't have hit Mum.'
- 'If hadn't lost my coat, then Mum wouldn't be crying.'

These children live with the contradiction they can feel both powerful and powerless. They may present in school as being hyper vigilant, noticing everything and being overly concerned with what is happening around them as a way of trying to manage their feelings of anxiety and fear. It can appear that they are not listening, but often they are able to listen and watch at the same time, and have developed this skill as a coping mechanism to help them live with and manage trying to get things right all the time.

Internal belief system

Children develop an internal belief system about themselves by the messages they receive from other people. These messages define whether they are lovable, valuable and worth listening to and spending time with and have a significant influence on a child's confidence, self-esteem, self-belief and how they feel about themselves.

Table 2.3 Developing a positive internal belief system

Parent behaviour	Child feels and internalises the message
Shares reading book with child	I am worth helping and I feel good about myself
Attends parents' open morning	Mum is interested in me and how I am doing at school
Praises child	I am a good person and I can do useful things
Asks child about their day	I am worth getting to know and how I feel is important
Helps child to manage conflict with sibling	Adults can help me

Dealing with contradictions

Families lay the foundations for a feeling of security and children bring their experience of this, or the lack of it, into school with them. The family is the place where children learn an initial code of conduct with guidelines, rules and expectations for behaviour. This code of conduct may be in conflict with the behavioural expectations of the school, resulting in the child having to navigate their way through a whole new set of rules. The dilemma for the child may be, 'Do I please my parents or my teacher?' Either way, this may mean going against or gaining disapproval from one of the significant adults in the child's life. This is particularly difficult for a child who is constantly trying to get it right and please other people, as they are stuck in a no-win situation.

The conflict between the different codes of conduct at home and at school may cause particular problems after school holidays, where the family will have had a much stronger influence over the child due to length of time spent with them. The more differences there are between home and school in terms of expectations and behaviour, the longer and more difficult it may be for the child to adjust to the return to school. If children come from families where things are chaotic and unsettled, rather than calm and peaceful, they may seek to create this at school as it is familiar to them.

Table 2.4 Conflicting messages between home and school

Child's behaviour	Response at home	Response at school
Persistently says 'no'	Adult gives child what they want	Child is given explanation and encouraged to participate
Has a tantrum	Adult ignores them	Child receives explanation about how to behave
Hits another child	Adult hits them	Child gets age-appropriate consequence
Swears	Adult laughs	Child has age-appropriate 'time out'
Interrupting adults	Adult talks louder or shouts	Child is reprimanded and reminded of school rules

If there are no rules or boundaries at home for the child's behaviour, or these are inconsistent and changeable, depending on how the parent feels at the time, the child will learn that life can be unpredictable and that adults can be manipulated and controlled at times. For these children, the world can be a very confusing and unsafe place, as the codes of conduct at home and school are incompatible. If a child has learned at home that if you challenge adults, plead for your own way and sulk if you don't get it, and adults give in to you, they will try this approach at school, with a very different result for their behaviour.

Child learns

- I can talk back to adults.
- I can do what I want when I want.
- I can manipulate adults to get my own way.
- I can shout when I want something.
- I can interrupt adults to get myself heard.
- I can ignore adults when I choose to.

If a child tries behaviour at school that produces a different outcome at home, it can be very upsetting and confusing for them if it doesn't achieve their desired result. Children who use manipulative, challenging and controlling behaviour at school may have learned to do this as a way of trying to create their own consistency in an inconsistent world. They are attempting to reproduce an experience that is familiar to them as a way of feeling safe. For example, a child who keeps getting up and wandering around when they are supposed to be sitting down at an activity.

Children who may have no rules or consequences for their behaviour at home and have lots of freedom may experience school as very restrictive. These children can live in a constant state of high anxiety and it may be difficult for them to manage even very small changes at school. They may refuse to do things and may be seen as being difficult, when they are actually trying to manage their high levels of anxiety caused by things changing. It is crucial that children who experience these difficulties are provided with a sense of predictability and routine and offered explanations as much as possible, in order to reduce their need to try and create this for themselves and allow them to feel safe and settled in school. However, children who come from families who use corporal punishment at home as a way of managing their child's behaviour may feel that the school is too soft, and this has a negative impact on the child's behaviour at school. Equally, the school may feel that the parents' approach is too harsh. The result is confusion and anxiety for the child who is caught between the two conflicting approaches.

Case study

Dylan, aged 4, came from a family where it was acceptable to swear at people when things felt frustrating or difficult. At school he would often swear at staff or other children if he could not have his own way. This resulted in him being reprimanded, asked to apologise and reminded of the school rules, which was very confusing for him.

When a child receives attention for negative behaviour, rather than positive, they may view themselves as negative. If a child doesn't get a response from an adult at home when they show or tell them something positive, it can reinforce the message that 'good' behaviour doesn't get a response but 'bad' behaviour does. This can result in the child feeling they need to display negative behaviour to be noticed and get adult attention. If they only receive attention for negative behaviour at home, then at school they receive attention for positive behaviour, they may not understand why the focus is different. A child that is noticed for their 'bad' behaviour rather than their 'good' may conclude that they are bad rather than good. It may reinforce the message that nothing about them is good. The contradictive response they receive at school may confuse them further: 'Am I bad or good? Dad thinks it's funny when I swear, but it makes Mrs Thompson very cross.' It can be an arduous task for schools to undo the early and external messages that children receive about themselves, and while they may be unable to do much to change the child's external world, they are able to change their internal world by providing them with an alternative image of themselves as a good person.

Getting it wrong

While it is developmentally appropriate for children aged 3–5 to want to be the biggest, the best and to win and go first at everything, this is hugely influenced by how this is dealt with in the child's family. The responses that children absorb from home about making mistakes can have a big influence on their school life on a daily basis. It can impact on a child's ability to try something new, to persevere with something they find difficult and to be honest about getting something wrong. When a child will not let an adult help them with something, their behaviour may indicate a very fragile sense of themselves. Equally, a child that lies may have learned that it is not safe enough to tell the truth and may be so adamant and highly skilled at lying that the member of staff starts to doubt themselves. For this child, the feelings of shame they experience may be overwhelming, hence the lying and determination not to be found out.

Case study

Marcel, aged 4, appeared to be enjoying being part of the friendship group at school. On the fourth week, he accidentally knocked over the model they were making together and immediately said the other child had done it. Although the group facilitator acknowledged that it had happened accidentally, he was still adamant he hadn't done it.

For Marcel, the possibility of getting something wrong was overwhelming, and he had learned that it was better to lie and pretend it was someone else than admit the truth. In his family he was often reprimanded and blamed for things his other siblings had done.

Marcel needs:

- opportunities to make mistakes and get things wrong with an adult on an individual basis who can acknowledge his feelings, e.g. 'It can feel awful when you get something wrong, but everyone makes mistakes sometimes';
- adults to acknowledge their own mistakes to him, e.g. 'I snapped my shoe laces this morning when I was putting my shoes on, but it's okay because accidents happen and I can buy new laces';
- positive responses to him making mistakes, e.g. 'You tried really hard to read that word, even though it was very difficult for you; it's okay to get things wrong. Well done for trying'.

When a child behaves in this way it can have a big impact on their learning and ability to make and sustain friendships with other children. Some children may also refuse to try new things for fear of getting things wrong and may have learned that feelings of adults being cross or disappointed with them are easier to manage than the fear of new experiences. These children need to feel safe to try new things without fear of being shamed or humiliated by adults.

Learning how to manage feelings

The reactions to feelings and how they are acknowledged and expressed within the family provide children with a template that they may replicate at school. As discussed in Chapter 1, self-regulation and the ability to identify and respond to feelings is learned in childhood and carried on into adulthood. Children learn self-regulation by having an adult who can help them to identify, name and express their feelings. Children learn this at a very young age, as babies' brains are still developing and are very sensitive to stress and they are unable to regulate their own stress and depend on their carers to regulate it for them. The way that adults respond to this stress can either soothe and alleviate it or exacerbate it. If they are responded to in a way that soothes it, they gradually develop their own stress management system. If they receive what they need they then become able to manage the stress more easily themselves. However, if the adult responds in a way that increases the stress, it can heighten the anxiety levels and prevent this development taking place. If children do not receive soothing from an adult in times of distress and upset, they do not develop their own stress-regulating system, unless another significant adult takes on these vital parental functions with the child on a regular basis. School staff can play a vital role in helping children learn to understand and express their feelings and therefore develop self-regulation.

When a child has not learned self-regulation, it can have an enormous impact on their learning and relationships at school. They may become involved in arguments and fights with other children and may be unable to accept or deal with the feelings evoked by this. This can also affect their ability to be able to focus and engage with their learning, as they may be preoccupied with trying to manage their feelings. Their inability to self-regulate may also affect their friendships with other children and relationships with school staff.

The way that the adults in the child's family respond to and demonstrate managing their own feelings impacts on how children learn to do this and the messages they receive about how acceptable this is. This may also be in conflict with school and the messages they receive there. For example, how do the child's parents express anger and frustration?

Table 2.5 Expressing feelings in the family

Situation	Feeling	Expressed by parent
Post office is closed	Anger	Punches the wall outside the shop
Can't open a jar	Frustration	Throws it across the room
Has an argument with a friend	Sadness	Gets drunk
Will be late for an appointment	Anxiety	Shouts and screams at the bus driver

All the above situations are terrifying for children who may learn that feelings are not good things to have and should be avoided. When children learn to hold on to their feelings and not express them, it can be very difficult for them to change this behaviour. They may develop a 'don't care' attitude to learning, friendships and school, which can be a learned response to avoiding having to deal with feelings. Children who have learned to suppress their feelings may believe that they should not have them and certainly should not show them.

The group work programmes are devised to enable children to practise identifying, understanding and expressing their feelings on a weekly basis with the support of a caring adult. This experience can enable the children to transfer this skill outside the group situation and to become more emotionally articulate. For example, while talking about feelings, Joe, aged four, said, 'I'm worried because my mum is sad.' His mum had periods of depression, and during this time she found it very hard to engage with and show any interest in him. By providing Joe with an experience to identify and talk about his feelings, he was able to start to understand them and to feel less scared and isolated.

Within the family children witness reactions to everyday events, and these may affect their responses to drama and excitement. If a child experiences excitement, drama and attention from everyday events involving relationships and conflict, they learn that drama is important and this is how to get a response from the adults around them. They may start to re-create this in school as it is familiar, and they may crave the adrenalin and excitement that dramatic events can provide; for example, a child who comes in from playing outside with a long and complicated story that involves lots of people and events. The teacher may not react in the way the child is expecting and therefore doesn't get the response they were looking for. The child may then proceed to create more drama by being disruptive to get the attention they are craving. They may become overly involved in what other people are doing and provide commentaries on it. They may find it hard to just stick to the facts in events and not add their own fabrication which they think may result in them getting more attention.

Parental expectations

Parents will bring their own experiences of schooling and their attitude towards education and learning with them in to school. It is essential that school staff are aware of this and the potential impact it can have on the parents' ability to fully engage with and support their child's learning. If a child's parents have negative experiences of school and staff from their own childhood, then it can take a great deal of courage to even walk through the school gates, let alone speak to teachers or approach the head teacher. If a child's parents are consistently avoiding entering the school, it can be useful to explore the possible reasons for this and offer alternative times to talk to them, if possible. There may be numerous reasons for this; for example, they may feel overwhelmed by the other parents, particularly if they experience them as loud and domineering.

Reflect: How do you experience parents?

Think about how you experience parents who are challenging or may be experiencing difficulties with school, and ask yourself if you would be happy to wait around in the playground talking to them?

Some parents may believe that school is a waste of time and that children don't learn anything. They may think that school staff are too strict or too soft and say things like, 'It never did me any good'. They may keep their children off school, not wake them up in the morning so the children are late, discourage them from doing their reading book and refuse to pay for school trips. These parents may find it more difficult to engage with the school and their child's learning and may require additional support from a family worker or attendance officer, if they are available at the school.

Case study

Emma was the parent of three children and had found her own school days to be very difficult, as she was extremely shy and had been bullied by a large group of girls for many years. She had experienced the school staff as only being interested in the bright and lively pupils, and after eventually finding the courage to tell one of them about being bullied, was dismissed as wasting the teacher's time. Emma then played truant regularly and stopped going all together on her sixteenth birthday. She had left school with no qualifications and wanted her own children to do well at school. She was mistrustful of all school staff and appeared aggressive and volatile at times. She would rush in, shout at the children to hurry up and then chase them out of the school building. The school staff thought she was rude and uninterested in her children's education, and were amazed that the children all produced their homework on time and had their reading records signed every night.

The parent's relationship with their child

A useful indicator of both a parent's relationship with school and their child is how they meet and greet each other at the start and end of the school day. Is the child brought to school by an older sibling or a parent who is always on the phone and pushes them through the door? Or are they brought to school by Mum or Dad who kisses them and tells them to have a good day? This start of the school day can impact enormously on the child's ability to settle in to class easily and engage with their learning. How are they greeted if they are collected by the parent at the end of the day? Are they acknowledged or met with scowls and reprimands such as 'What's that on your jumper?'

If the child shows the parent a certificate or picture they have made, does the parent respond or just carry on talking to another parent or continue their conversation on their mobile phone? All these responses provide children with messages about how loved, valued and important they are.

If a parent is critical and judgemental towards their child, the child learns, 'I am not good enough, I can't get it right, it's not okay to be me, and there must be something wrong with me'. These can all have a strong impact on their self-esteem and self-worth and over time may gradually erode their sense of self. When a child feels worthless, this can lead to a sense of hopelessness and despair. If a child feels unloved and unlovable as a result of the messages they receive, they may seek external gratification through food, bullying others, and being demanding and clingy to school staff as a way to manage their feelings. This can all have a significant impact on the child's behaviour.

Table 2.6 Development of internal belief system

Child feels	Child learns	Child behaves
I'm not good enough	I am worthless	Tries to make other people happy
I can't get it right	I need to try harder	Tries to be perfect
It's not okay to make mistakes	I need to be perfect	Is bossy, manipulative, controlling
It's not okay to be me	I need to be different/someone else	Is always putting other people's needs before their own

Additional pressures on parents

The external difficulties that some parents may be dealing with on a daily basis may result in them not being able to meet the emotional needs of their children, however much they may want to. The impact of situations such as domestic violence, poverty, bereavement, poor housing and drug and alcohol dependency may all result in a parent being stressed, anxious and preoccupied with their own problems. This may mean they are physically and/or emotionally unavailable for the child and may find it difficult to engage with the child's emotional needs. When a parent is stressed, they may have no capacity to understand or meet the child's feelings, as they can be too overwhelmed by their own. The parent may want to be able to do this for their child, but their own practical and emotional difficulties may be barriers to them being able to do this. Unfortunately, when children are living in circumstances like this, they can respond to the anxiety and stress by becoming more insecure and anxious themselves, creating another stress for the parent to manage.

Case study

Margaret had five children and was frequently complaining about the school and the way her children were treated. The school staff found her challenging and would turn round and start walking the other way if they saw her in the corridor, rather than face the torrent of negativity she sometimes had waiting for them. Since her youngest child had started full time at the school nursery, Margaret had found her days long and empty. She was at her happiest during the school holidays or if one of the children was unwell and had to stay at home with her.

The head teacher approached Margaret and asked her if she would be willing to help organise and repair books in the school library with another parent, as the school staff were struggling to find the time to do this. Margaret resisted at first but eventually agreed to 'give it a go'. The role created for her by the head teacher made her feel important, valued and that she had a purpose. She became more positive towards the school, seemed happier in herself and eventually started working as a lunchtime organiser.

The opportunity provided by this school enabled Margaret to realise she had something to offer, and was able to contribute and receive attention in a positive way. It also enabled her to use her skills as a parent to find work.

The impact of domestic violence on children

When a child is living in a stressful situation, such as domestic violence, their home can become a terrifying and unpredictable place, rather than a haven of security. The significant impact on children of living in these circumstances and – the enormity of the problem – can be hard to comprehend. A child may be preoccupied with what is happening at home and unable to engage with their learning. They may have difficulty retaining information and appear to be in their own world a lot of the time. If children live with fear, it may affect their ability to hear instructions; for example, a child just standing staring into space as they are unable to remember what they have been asked to do.

Some children may have negative associations of mealtimes, as this may be when the violence occurs, and they may either eat very fast to get away from the situation or pretend they are not hungry. They may have learned to accept feeling hungry as mealtimes at home are often disrupted by fights and violence. A child who has experienced domestic violence may also come across as being very vigilant, as they may have learned to be watchful as a way of trying to stay safe. Living with domestic violence may result in some children finding it difficult to make friends and manage relationships, due to confusion over what is acceptable and unacceptable behaviour. They may become quiet and withdrawn or become loud and fidgety with poor concentration. They may feel angry, confused, anxious, insecure and frightened. This may result in them having nightmares, being more tired than usual due to disturbed or lack of sleep.

Children who grow up in a family where there is domestic violence may learn powerful lessons about the use of control, intimidation and force in relationships. They can learn that aggression is part of everyday life and it is acceptable to shout at and hit other people. This can make it very confusing and difficult when they are at school, where this behaviour is not seen as acceptable. They may try to placate school staff, as they have learned to try and please other people as a way of trying to control the situation. Children who live with domestic violence may not experience positive relationships being modelled, as they may have one parent who is the controlling aggressor and the other parent who is the terrified victim. This may make it hard for either parent to be consistently physically or emotionally available for the child, resulting in the family being a very frightening place at times. It is essential that these children are provided with help and support to manage their peer relationships in school so they avoid replicating the controlling behaviours they have experienced.

Case study

Shakira, aged 5, had witnessed domestic violence several times during the last three years. At school she was often hitting the other children and saying hurtful things to them. Her class teacher spent some time with her explaining the impact of her behaviour on the other children and helped her to think of some kind things she could say to them instead. She took Shakira round the class while the children were involved in their activities and encouraged her to practise saying kind words to them and asked the children to each tell her how that made them feel.

This positive experience enabled Shakira to practise a new way of relating to the children with support from an adult.

Managing transitions

For most children, starting school and managing daily school life with its challenges and changes along with moving to a new class at the end of each school year is enough to deal with. However, some children may also be starting school without the experience of being in the nursery class at the school and therefore have an even bigger adjustment to make. For these children, it can be even more difficult to adjust to being at school, as friendships may already have been made within the year group. This may impact on their ability to settle at school, adapt to the structure of the school day, and integrate with the rest of the class.

Staff strategy – helping a child settle

Identify a key person to be allocated to any new child to help them settle in to the class and the school. Allow them as much choice as possible and allow them to build relationships with children and staff gradually, in their own time and at their own pace.

The wider community

Just as there can be differences between the code of conduct at home and school, this can be reinforced by the wider community that children are living in. There can be hierarchies of power between families and this experience may result in people living in fear. For example, an adult being scared to report the domestic violence they hear from their neighbours every night for fear of reprisals. There may be a different moral code that children are dealing with that may conflict with school. For example, a child who is asked not to lie, cheat or steal at school, but knows that their mum puts nappies in the bottom of the pushchair and walks out of the shop without paying for them. This child can be in conflict about what is right and wrong and may be unclear about how to get it right themselves. Is it okay to steal food if you are hungry or take nappies if you haven't got any money?

Schools face an enormous task of trying to change some of the behaviours that are aspired to and validated by the wider community in some areas. The way in which status and power are achieved and recognised in some communities may be very different from the experience that schools are trying to encourage children to develop. Is it good to be clever or do you have to be naughty to be noticed? It is a complex task to try and understand the impact this can have on children in terms of who they are and the expectations and code of conduct from the community versus school. There are different gender pressures on girls and boys, and these can be in conflict with who the child is and the strengths and abilities the school is actively encouraging the child to pursue. For example, a boy who excels at singing or dance may not be encouraged by his family or the community to pursue this talent. The child can be caught in a conflict of trying to gain approval from three external areas.

Some schools are operating in communities where there may be three or more generations of the same family living there who have never worked. The children in the family may never have known a family member who has worked. This can be in direct contrast to the messages of the school about working hard. How do we encourage children to integrate this message without saying that school is right and their family is wrong?

It can be very hard to develop aspirations, determination and motivation to succeed, along with a sense of purpose and having goals for children who may have only experienced the opposite outside school. It can be difficult to inspire children to be the best of who they are and reach their full potential when it may conflict so strongly with the messages of their family and wider community. It is our responsibility to help generations of families to break this cycle.

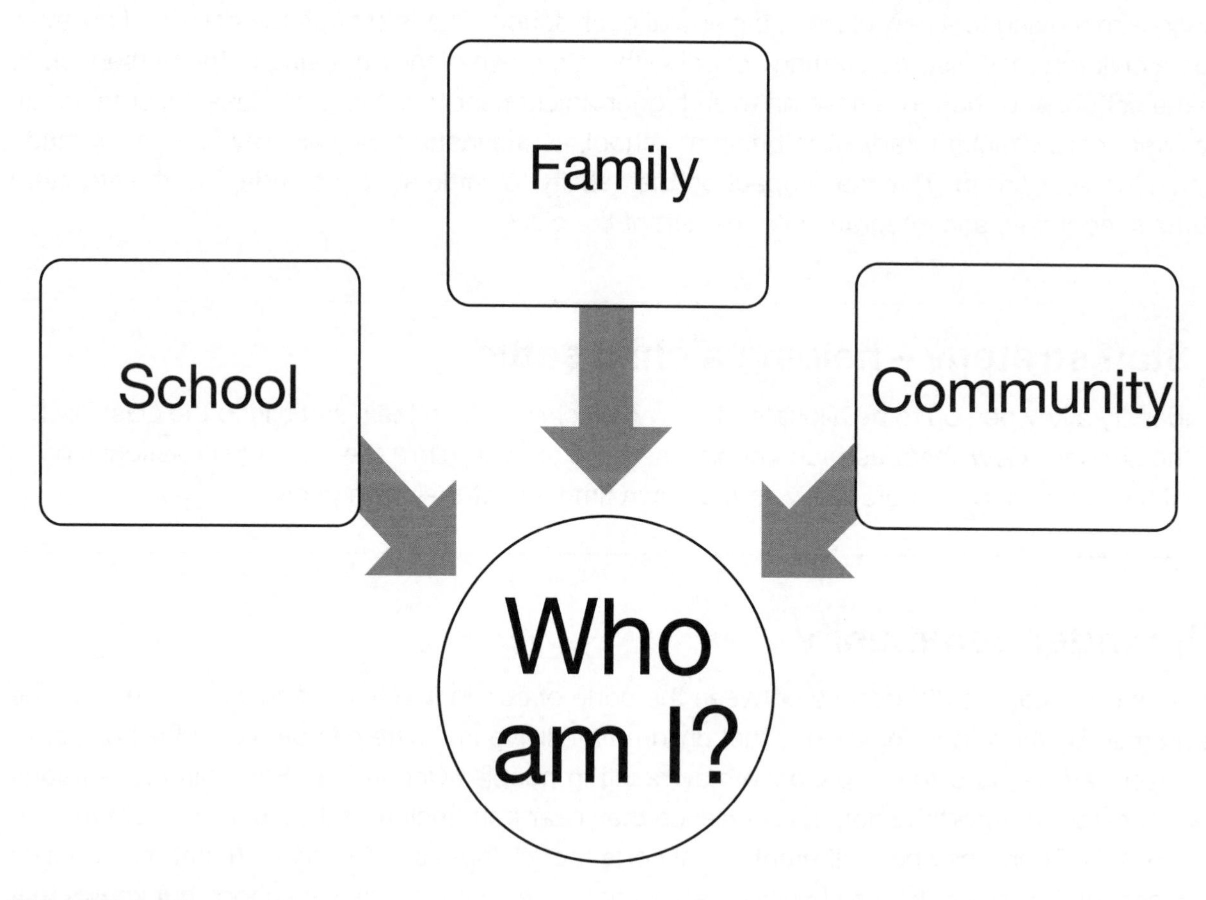

Figure 2.1 Who am I?

3 What is this child trying to tell me?

Every child wants to be seen, known, valued and understood, but, sadly, for some children their behaviour can result in them getting the opposite of what they need. If a child is being disruptive, being uncooperative and challenging school staff, or if a child is constantly trying to please other people, they are very clearly trying to communicate something to the adults around them. Most adults use language to express their needs and how they feel to other people. Most children, however, do not have the same language skills as adults and use behaviour to communicate their feelings. They need help from sensitive adults to help them work out and express what they feel. Every behaviour is trying to tell us something; for example, a tantrum may be communicating fear, frustration, boredom or anger. A child who is disruptive and challenging to school staff may be ensuring that he gets noticed and is not forgotten about or overlooked. It is the adult's role to try and understand what the child may be trying to tell them and then to respond accordingly.

How adults and children communicate

Reflect: Compare the two scenarios:

Scenario 1

You are a class teacher for Reception and you had an argument with your partner before you left for work this morning, resulting in you arriving at school late and unprepared.

- How easy would you find it to settle at work and perform well?
- What would you be thinking and feeling?
- What could you do about this?
- How could you communicate your feelings and get support?

Scenario 2

You are 5 years old and your mum was very cross with you before you left for school this morning, resulting in you arriving late to school without your reading book.

- How easy would you find it to settle in to class and engage with your learning?
- What would you be thinking and feeling?
- What could you do about this?
- How could you communicate your feelings and get support?

Sometimes, as adults, we can forget that we have the benefit of experience, developed language skills and the ability to articulate our thoughts and feelings if we choose to. We are able to rationalise experiences and know that we will survive them. We have strategies to solve difficult situations and the benefit of life experiences to know that things usually pass and life does not stay challenging forever. We can choose to talk to people and get support, if and when we need it. How difficult are any of these for a 5-year-old or even younger child to do? Is it therefore surprising that they communicate their feelings and need for support through their behaviour? As adults, the more understanding we can have of what a child may be trying to communicate to us through their behaviour, the greater the chance of the child being understood and being able to make sense of their thoughts and feelings, and the more compassion adults can have for them. Children are often very alone with overwhelming thoughts and feelings, and this can be a lonely and terrifying experience.

Children communicate a range of different feelings through their behaviour, and these can be expressed in many different ways; for example, if a child is scared they may hide under the table or pretend they are not bothered.

Table 3.1 Understanding behaviour

Behaviour	Possible feeling
Hiding under table	Scared
Following adult around school	Lonely
Throwing objects	Angry
Hitting someone	Frustrated
Fiddling with something	Anxious
Challenging an adult	Terrified
Criticising another child	Jealous
Putting their head down	Embarrassed
Chewing their jumper	Worried

A child who clings to their parent or gets distressed when they try to leave them at school is trying to tell us something and it is the role of school staff to try and work out what they need. The child may be communicating that they are scared or anxious and they need support and reassurance to help them manage their feelings of distress and become calm. Sometimes, parents or school staff may assume the best thing to do in this situation is for the parent to leave, but this will often increase the child's distress and cause high levels of anxiety. It is better for the parent to spend time with them and encourage them to settle at an activity or with a friend, as this will ease their separation. If the child's behaviour is responded to with patience and understanding, it may enable the child to be settled more easily.

Staff strategy – to help a child who is finding it hard to separate

- Ask the parent to bring in a small object from home or a hanky that smells of them.
- Acknowledge to the child that it can make us feel sad when we have to leave Mum/Dad etc. and explain that this can make it easier to do this.
- Allow the child to have the object whenever they need it and trust that they will stop using it when they are more settled.

Children's internal dialogue

Some children may have learned to respond in a defensive way as a coping mechanism to manage the feelings of anxiety and fear that situations evoke in them. The child may present as feeling the opposite of this; for example, not scared and not bothered, but he may have learned to do this as a way of not feeling pain: 'If I pretend I don't care, then I can't be hurt or feel pain.' For this child, the silent pain of feeling unwanted or unloved can result in them feeling isolated, confused, frightened and alone. They may feel that everything that happens is their fault and have an internal dialogue that asks, 'Am I a bad person? Am I unlovable? Why do I get it wrong all the time? Why can't I do anything right?' When children have this internal belief system and are convinced that they do not deserve anything good, they may go to extreme lengths to prove it.

The combination of their feelings of low self-worth, along with a negative internal dialogue, may, not surprisingly result in challenging and disruptive behaviour as the child tries to bury their feelings and silence their internal voice. They may also actively try to sabotage situations to re-create the feelings and experiences that are familiar to them. Children who have a negative internal dialogue may believe that adults do not like them when they reprimand them. These children may find it difficult to hold on to positive thoughts about themselves, as they do not have an internal view of themselves as a good person. School staff can play an essential role in helping to rewrite their internal scripts into a positive dialogue. For example, 'If Mrs Hawkins thinks I'm a kind person, maybe I am.' It is crucial that we focus on the positives for these children, no matter how hard this may be to implement and sustain.

Case study

Nathan, aged 5, was often late for school and would shout at school staff and run off when challenged about his behaviour. He found it difficult to manage any relationships with the other children as he was unpredictable and would lash out and hit them, often laughing as he did this. The school staff were finding his behaviour very difficult to manage and were also concerned about his physical safety, as he would sometimes hide around the school.

Possible reasons for Nathan's behaviour:

- His dad had died recently and his mum was finding it hard to cope with him and his younger sister.
- Nathan was terrified that his mum might die, too, and he did not know how to express his feelings.
- He was worried about his mum when he was at school because she kept crying all the time and was very sad.

When children show us behaviour that can be challenging and difficult to manage, it can be hard to consider that behind the behaviour may be feelings of fear and terror. Children such as Nathan may be easily misunderstood in our schools and it can be a complex task to try and understand the possible feelings behind the behaviour. It can be difficult to imagine a child may be feeling fragile and vulnerable when their behaviour appears to be showing us the opposite of this. It can be a challenge for adults to look beyond the child's behaviour and see the pain underneath. If a child is demonstrating difficult and unmanageable behaviour, they may be showing us that they are having difficult and unmanageable feelings and that they need help with them.

Responding to behaviour

Children do not want negative comments or attention for challenging behaviour, but some children may have learned that any attention is better than no attention and therefore may evoke negative reactions from adults. Children who seek attention in the form of disapproval because they believe they will not gain attention in the form of approval may be showing us they have low self-esteem and may believe that other people are unable to see the good in them. For example, a child that constantly calls out in class may be doing this to ensure that they stay noticed. It is a guaranteed way of ensuring that they receive attention and are remembered. This may tell us about the child's experiences outside school: Why do they need to ensure that they are noticed and remembered at school? Do they have a different experience at home? When children are happy and settled they do not need to ensure that adults notice and remember them; if they do this it is an indication that they need additional help and support.

It can be hard for some children to tolerate their feelings and this can result in them trying to get rid of them rather than accepting and trying to understand and process them. For example, a child who is unable to manage feeling angry may hit another child or throw something as a way of trying to get rid of that feeling. When a child picks on or bullies another child, it may make them feel big and powerful and can be an opportunity for them to feel strong, albeit for a short amount of time. Children need help and support from adults to realise that it is natural to have feelings and that they can be helped to understand how to recognise and express them. It can be useful to talk about feelings regularly throughout the day and make appropriate references to them; for example, 'It can make us feel sad when it's raining and we can't play outside.' This validates their experiences and normalises how children may be feeling. Some children have little resilience to cope with their feelings, and events that can happen during the course of a school day can feel too difficult for them to manage, such as waiting to have a turn on a bike or not being at the front of the line. Experiences such as these can be interpreted by children to mean that they are special, important and good enough. For children who have a fragile sense of themselves it can feel overwhelming to imagine someone else being chosen to do something instead of them. This is particularly difficult for 3- and 4-year-olds (and also some 5-year-olds), where developmentally they may still be finding it hard to cooperate and share; it is useful if they are able to have some preparation for this. The following activity can help children to develop independence and build resilience.

Staff strategy – to help children who find it difficult to wait their turn

Use a clock or timer to show when things will be happening. For example, when the big hand gets to '6', then it will be your turn to play in the water.

For school staff it can be a huge challenge to look beyond the behaviour and attempt to understand what the child may be feeling. It can be easy to judge children for their behaviour, as the following comments demonstrate:

- He's just attention seeking.
- She just wants her own way.
- He never stops talking.
- She's such a good child.

- He's so helpful.
- She's so immature.
- He never speaks.
- She never listens.

However, if adults are able to meet a child's need to be noticed and remembered in a positive and supportive way, they may reduce or even stop the behaviour. For example, 'I know it's really hard for you to sit quietly, so why don't you sit next to me so I can help you.' For young children, simply coping with the expectations of the school day can be difficult to manage, especially if they are not used to having a routine or have not had the experience of sitting quietly at home.

Staff strategy – helping a child to sit quietly

Explain to the child that you are going to help them to practise not talking and show them that you will be pointing to their mouth when you would like them to not talk. Practise this one to one with the child before carpet time. Sit the child near to you so they are able to see you and repeat the action when necessary.

This activity keeps the child focusing on you and can help to reduce their anxiety. It may also meet their need to be noticed as they have a connection to the adult along with the acknowledgement of their efforts and achievements.

What are children trying to communicate?

When children show us their feelings through their behaviour it is important that we not only try to understand what they may be feeling and trying to communicate to us, but also that we provide them with an emotional vocabulary to help them to talk about their experiences. For example, when a child says they do not want to do something, they may be telling us they are scared or anxious. How often as adults may we decide we don't want to do something when the real reason may be that we are scared? It can be useful to respond by saying, 'I know you are saying that you don't want to do that, but sometimes it can feel a bit frightening to try new things.' If a child uses a baby voice to ask for something or talk to us, they may be telling us they are feeling small and vulnerable. It can be helpful to consider what the emotional age of the child is and whether it would be useful to respond as you would with a younger child. When a child fidgets, rocks on their chair, taps things or wriggles on the carpet, they are again telling us something. It may be they are telling us they feel worried, anxious or stressed. A response such as, 'I can see you are finding it hard to stay still at the moment,' can be enough to help a child relax, as it communicates that you have noticed them without reprimanding them. It is also important to consider the child's non-verbal communication, such as their breathing: is it shallow or does it quicken when they are asked to do certain tasks?

Young children have not been using verbal language for very long, and as a result of this and their cognitive understanding they may find it very difficult to be able to put their feelings into words. Tantrums can be triggered by a child feeling overwhelmed and frightened by their feelings; for example, fear, frustration and disappointment can all be experienced very intensely, without the emotional vocabulary to express them and ask for support. Therefore, it is crucial that they are provided with regular opportunities during the school day to help them to link the feelings with the appropriate language to describe it.

Staff strategy – find the feeling

To help children to identify how they feel, the use of a 'feelings board' at regular intervals during the day can help them. Explain and give examples of what each feeling means. Draw a face under the word in each box to show the feeling and attach an arrow with a paper fastener in the middle of the square. Ask the child to move the arrow to the relevant feeling.

Happy	Sad
Angry	Scared

This can help children to connect with their feelings more easily and provide permission for the child to experience all their feelings as acceptable. It can also provide a useful stepping stone for children who need more support with linking facial expressions with actual feelings.

Helping children to reconnect

Children who live in noisy and chaotic families may tune out and be in their own world as a way of finding some internal peace. At school they may appear not to be listening and may seem disengaged and uninterested. If a child has developed this behaviour as a coping strategy in order to make it easier to live with chaos, we need to be supportive of this and ensure we approach it sensitively. For example, gentle reminders such as a tap on the arm can help them to reconnect with the present moment. The school staff's increased awareness of the possible reasons behind children's behaviour can ensure they offer the appropriate support for the situation. For example, if a child says they feel unwell on a regular basis, it may be an indication of stress or anxiety. Children may find it hard to differentiate between physical and emotional pain: they just know they do not feel well. Expressions such as 'sick with fear' are realistic for children who do not have the emotional vocabulary or understanding to separate physical from emotional discomfort.

Table 3.2 Links between physical and emotional well-being

Physical feeling	Possible emotional reason
Headache	Worry
Sickness	Fear
Stomach ache	Anxiety

Children may create their own rituals that they demonstrate at school to enable them to feel secure, such as going to the toilet at a particular time of the day or having to sit on the same chair. This behaviour may indicate anxiety and fear and will only be alleviated when the child feels safer. Wherever possible, unless it impacts on another child, it will help the child if this behaviour can be accepted and attention given to helping them feel settled and secure, rather than trying to change their behaviour.

Children who either hurt themselves and cry for a long time and find it hard to be comforted, or children who do not seek comfort or show any distress when they have been hurt can both be indicating a need for further support. If a child has learned to self-soothe, it may be that the adults have not been physically or emotionally available to help them with their feelings. It can be helpful to acknowledge this by saying, 'In school there are lots of adults who care for you; you can always tell us if you are hurt and we will try and make it better.' This provides a strong message to the child that the adults will help them and look after them.

Staff strategy – feeling settled

Offer an object such as a small figure or animal to the child to look after during the day and keep at school. This can help a child to feel more settled and safer at school. Encourage them to give it a name if they wish, to provide them with a sense of ownership.

The object can also be offered to children who are usually settled and happy at school but are dealing with a change of circumstance at home, such as moving house or the arrival of a new baby. The additional comfort offered by the object may help them to adjust to the change more easily and manage their feelings of fear and anxiety.

Some children may be emotionally immature due to poor relational experiences outside school that can impact on their social development, and they may find it harder to develop relationships with other children and school staff. Stress within the family may also result in the parent being less emotionally available for the child; for example, a child who has an alcohol- or drug-dependent parent may experience the parent's behaviour abruptly changing from affectionate and loving to angry and critical. This can create anxiety and stress for the child and may result in them expecting school staff to be unpredictable in their behaviour, too. For these children, a positive and consistent relational experience with an adult in school can enable them to build and maintain a connection, enabling them to access all aspects of school life more easily.

The cycle of misunderstanding

Case study

Dylan, aged 4, always pushed his way to the front of the dinner queue, knocking other children out of the way and hurting them in the process. This resulted in him being reprimanded, asked to apologise and spending lunchtimes on his own as the other children avoided him. Dylan's behaviour resulted in him not getting any of his needs met, as he had to go to the back of the queue and wait even longer for his lunch. He felt lonely and sad as the other children did not want to play with him.

Possible reasons for Dylan's behaviour:

- He never had breakfast at home as things were chaotic.
- He panicked that there wouldn't be enough food for him if he wasn't at the front of the line.
- He was so overwhelmed by his hunger, as he hadn't eaten, that he had no awareness of the other children.
- He wasn't able to say that he was really hungry and was terrified that he may have to go without food.

How often in schools do we see scenarios like this where children are trying to show us what they need or how they feel and they are misunderstood and they get the opposite of what they need? The cycle of misunderstanding demonstrates an all-too-common scenario in schools.

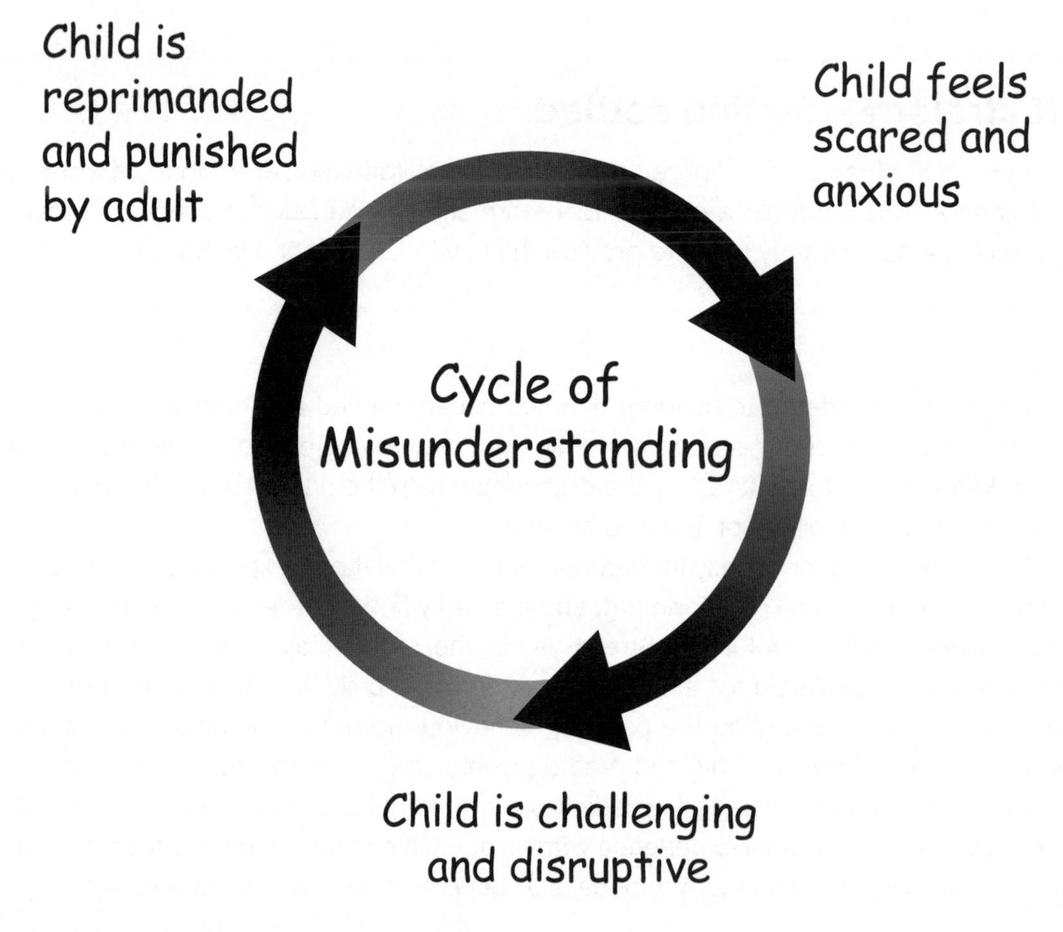

Figure 3.1 The cycle of misunderstanding

As has been discussed previously, for some children the contrast between behavioural expectations at home and school is huge. The conflict between acceptable behaviour at school is incompatible with acceptable behaviour at home. The norms of behaviour and morality that are developed at home can be poles apart from what is required at school and many children struggle hugely with this, only to be left with a sense of alienation as they get it wrong once again.

Children learn to develop their own coping strategies to manage their anxiety, and this can manifest itself in different ways, from being disruptive and aggressive to being withdrawn and shut down. It can be a challenge for school staff to try and work out what the possible reasons for the child's behaviour are, as well as trying to work out the best way to deal with it. The child's behaviour can often result in an outcome that increases their anxiety, rather than reduces it. It can be useful to consider where the child is emotionally, rather than developmentally, as this can help to understand some of their behaviour, which may be more appropriate for a child of a younger age.

Table 3.3 What is this behaviour telling us?

Behaviour	What the child has learned
Class clown	I've learned that I need to get people to notice me and make them laugh and use humour to get them to like me
Bossy	I've learned that I need to control things such as people, objects and tasks in order to feel safe
Perfectionist	I've learned that I need to get things right, it's not okay to make mistakes and I need to do things in a particular way to feel safe
Bully	I've learned that I need to make other people feel bad in order to make myself feel better because I think I am a bad person
Disengaged	I've learned that being in my own head and in my own world is familiar and the safest place to be
Fidgety	I've learned that fiddling with things helps me to feel safe and I feel scared and anxious when I can't do this

The above examples provide possible reasons why children have learned particular behaviours as coping strategies to deal with their feelings. If a child needs to have an object to play with or brings in an object from home, it enables school staff to develop a greater understanding of how the child feels. Children who bring in objects from home may be telling us they need help to feel safe at school. If a child was able to put those feelings into words, it would be easier for adults to empathise and support them.

Case study

Kane, aged 5, had frequent tantrums in class if he couldn't get his own way. He would snap pencils and damage other equipment, attack other children verbally and destroy his own work. After the tantrums, he would sit with his head in his hands and sob.

Possible reasons for Kane's behaviour:

- He had witnessed domestic violence between his parents for most of his life, resulting in him operating at an emotionally younger age.
- He felt scared and unsafe if he wasn't in control.
- He had learned to use controlling and bullying as a way to manage his anxiety.

Kane's teacher was encouraged to reflect on the possible reasons behind the behaviour while maintaining clear and firm boundaries with him: 'I can see that you are getting really cross – you look furious – but it's not okay to hurt other people. We need to find another way for you to have your feelings and not hurt anyone.' This response provides a clear message to Kane that he is important. The teacher is validating rather than dismissing his feelings and is offering him support with expressing them, therefore breaking the cycle of misunderstanding.

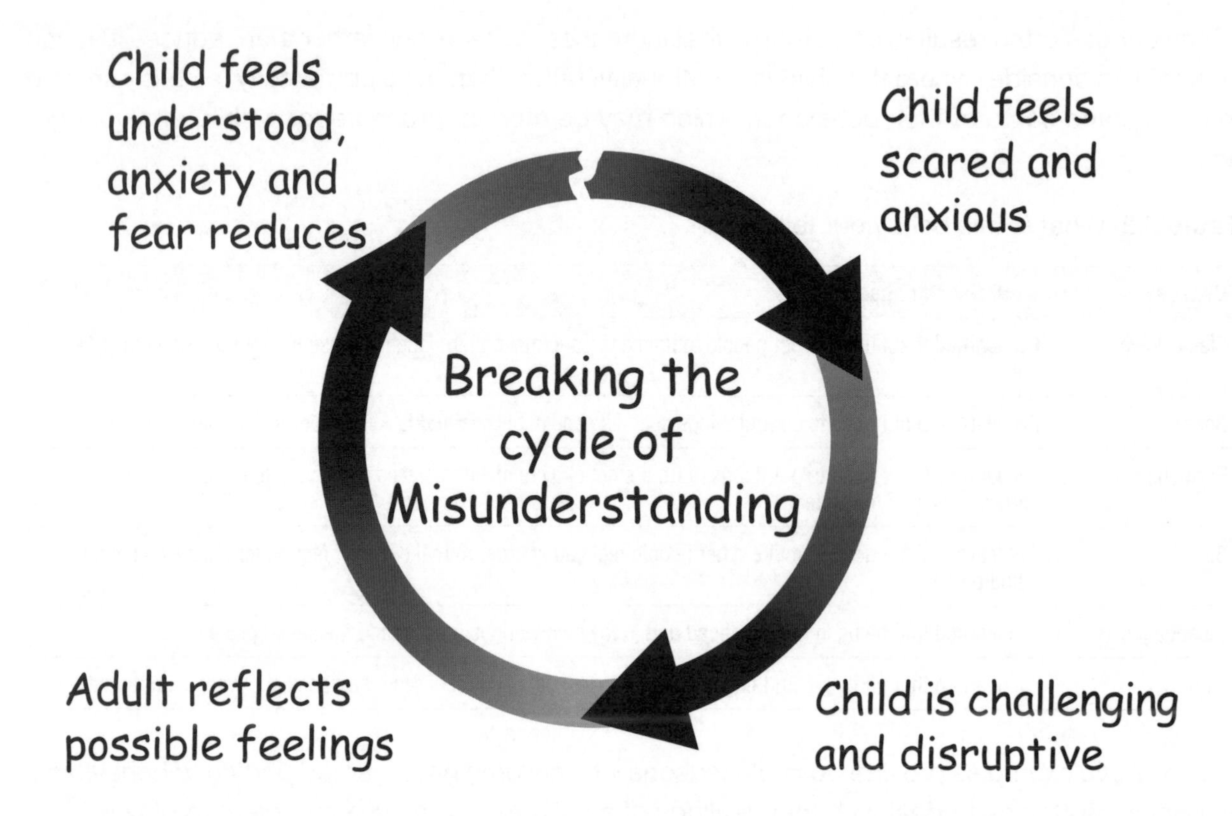

Figure 3.2 Breaking the cycle of misunderstanding

Using reflective language

Throughout this chapter and the rest of the book, I provide examples of ways of using reflective language. Reflective language conveys to the child that you are seeing them, trying to understand them and acknowledging any feelings they may be experiencing. It enables adults to tentatively explore the child's experience without making judgements or assumptions about it. Using reflective language clearly communicates to a child: 'I see you, I hear you, I am trying to understand you', and enables them to feel seen, heard, valued and understood. For some children this can be a relatively new experience and may result in increased self-worth and self-esteem.

Reflective language is a core concept of the group work programme and is key to its success. By using this with children, adults are providing a positive message to them: 'You are worth thinking about and trying to understand; I am trying to help you to work out how you feel and support you with understanding and managing your feelings.' It can be beneficial to use reflective language rather than always reprimanding children or telling them what to do, because it acknowledges and validates the child's feelings and experiences.

Case study

Oliver, aged 4, was very loud and talkative during the first session of the friendship group. The facilitator explained that he kept interrupting and talking over her and the other children in the group and also found it very hard to sit still.

Possible reasons for Oliver's behaviour:

- His home life was unpredictable with no structure or routine.
- He had three teenage siblings and the house was often very busy and loud.
- He wasn't able to say that he felt scared and anxious when he didn't know what was going to happen next.

I explained to the teaching assistant that he was probably very anxious about what would be happening in the group, along with being worried that he would not get a chance to talk. I encouraged her to acknowledge to him how hard it can be when you don't know what is going to happen and to reflect, 'I can see that it's really difficult for you to sit still and relax until you know what we are going to do.' This reflection gave a strong and positive message to Oliver that he was worth thinking about and trying to understand. I also suggested she acknowledge it was hard for him to wait and to reflect, 'It can be really hard to listen and wait for your turn to talk, but we can practise that in here and you will always have your time to talk.' Oliver responded well to this and relaxed as the sessions progressed. I encouraged the teaching assistant to share the process with his class teacher to raise her awareness of how he may behave when he is feeling anxious and to encourage her to use the same reflections with him in class to help him.

Children who find it difficult to show their feelings

This can occur when children have learned to internalise rather than externalise their feelings. It can make it more difficult for them to cope at school and to build friendships. They may present as quiet and withdrawn or uncaring and find it hard to show any emotion. Their facial expression may remain the same throughout the day as the events and circumstances around them change; for example, a child who shows no remorse when they have hurt another child and appears to have no understanding of other people's feelings. It can be very difficult for a child to understand other people's feelings if they have little or no understanding of their own. A child who finds it hard to show feelings may also have learned to bury their physical pain along with their emotional discomfort. They may have learned that no matter how much something hurts, it is not safe to make a fuss or ask for help.

Children who feel unsafe

In order for children to achieve any success at school, they need to feel both physically and emotionally safe. While this is essential for any child, if a child experiences their world outside school as unsafe, they may be vigilantly looking for evidence that the same is true at school. They may present at school as children who are eager to please and are constantly trying to work out what to do and what to say in order to get it right and please other people. In class they may be noticeable for their attentiveness, as they can often be watching everything that is happening. They may be the last person to carry out an instruction because they are watching what everyone else is doing first in order to make sure they get it right and to ensure that the adult meant what they said. For example, the class are asked to line up by the door and they are still sitting on the carpet. This child needs support with this and is not deliberately being slow or difficult. They are communicating their need to check things out all the time, and a gentle reminder of what they need to do can help with their anxiety about this. For example, 'I can see you are watching the other children line up, Emily, and maybe you need to check that is what we want you to do so you can get it right.'

Staff strategy – to help a child who can't retain instructions

Give children one instruction at a time and praise them after each one to help them manage their anxiety about forgetting.

This type of behaviour can also be common in children that are so scared and anxious that they are unable to retain much information in their head. This may present itself as a child that is in their own world, not listening and disengaged. They may have their own anxiety-filled internal dialogue in their head, which may be punctuated with lots of 'what if' terrifying scenarios. The life experiences for children who demonstrate this behaviour may have been filled with real, terrifying scenarios, and so their experience of the world is that awful things are always happening. You may get glimpses of a child's anxieties, especially around periods of change. For example, when a member of staff is absent they may keep asking where they are, even though you have told them several times. This snapshot into their internal world can help us understand how unsafe they feel and to witness their extreme levels of anxiety. They need to be met with patience, support, understanding and reassurance to help contain some of their feelings for them.

Some children appear to be well behaved and compliant, and may have developed this approach as a way of avoiding disapproval. For these children, the thought of upsetting other people is terrifying and they have learned to ignore or bury their needs and please others first. They can appear to be extremely well behaved and 'no trouble' at school. They may feel that other people would not like them if they showed their true selves, so present a way of behaving that they think other people will like and approve of. These children benefit greatly from being involved in the group work programmes, where all aspects of who they are are validated and accepted.

Children who display controlling behaviour

The reasons why a child may display controlling behaviour are many and varied. A child who bullies other children may be being bullied, dominated and controlled at home. They may be witnessing behaviour outside school that demonstrates to them how to control and manipulate other people. For example, a child who has controlling parents who do not allow the child to make any decisions or to have any choice or control over anything in their life, may also demonstrate this behaviour at school. A child who bullies other children needs help to find other ways to feel powerful and good about themselves. It is useful to explore how the child may feel about themselves, as children with confidence and self-esteem who feel good about themselves do not need or want to bully other children.

Children who demonstrate controlling behaviour towards other children, such as trying to turn other children against them or manipulating them into doing what they want them to, need the opportunity to experience success in other, more positive ways. Children bring their own experiences of success and failure, fairness and justice with them to school, which, depending on how these match the school experience, may impact on their behaviour. When a child experiences conflict between these two experiences from home and school, it can make it very hard for them to manage the differences, and this is explored in more detail in Chapter 2. If a child is constantly challenging school staff it is an indication that they need help to build and sustain relationships. This is discussed in more detail in Chapter 5.

Children who have difficulty communicating

When a child finds it hard to communicate, they need additional support to articulate their needs. If a child has English as a second language or is a selective mute, it is essential they are provided with the tools to help them to express their thoughts, needs and feelings. From the child's perspective, school life may be very frightening and confusing, and these feelings may manifest themselves in their behaviour. If a child chooses not to speak at school, it is important to work on helping to reduce their anxiety rather than focusing on how to get them to talk. There are also some children in our schools who need extra support with their communication skills due to talking late, having specific speech problems or perhaps still using a dummy when they are not at school. It is essential that these children are provided with extra help to support their language development.

Staff strategy – helping a child who chooses not to speak at school

- Explore using picture cards to help them communicate their needs, e.g. water bottle, toilet, etc.
- Encourage them to choose a job to do in class with another child to help build relationships with other children.

Children who need help managing their feelings

When children are having tantrums and are raging, their bodies are having a physical response, which can exacerbate the situation if it is not responded to appropriately by an adult. Some children fight with others or throw things when they are anxious or scared, others will try and hide or run off. The reactions can either be fight, wanting to fight against the feelings and bodily sensations, or flight, wanting to run away from them. Children who try to leave the class and/or hide are clearly communicating that they need help with their feelings. They may be saying, 'I feel overwhelmed, terrified and unsafe, and I need help to stop feeling like this.' If we respond to this behaviour by bringing the child back to class or out from under the table without helping them with their feelings, we are almost guaranteed that things will deteriorate as the day goes on. A response such as, 'I can see it is hard for you to stay in class/why you want to hide. I wonder if you are feeling worried – maybe you would like to look after the class teddy for a while?' may diffuse the situation more easily. If there is another adult available, they could also help them do a job if they would like to; sometimes being in the proximity of a caring adult can help to decrease the child's anxiety levels.

When a child has had help managing their feelings, they may feel safer and be able to access their learning again, rather than their anxiety and fear increasing and their behaviour deteriorating.

Children who have difficulty regulating stress may find it hard to tolerate excitement, resulting in them sabotaging events such as a school trip or Christmas party. In order to help children with this, it is necessary to understand the feelings behind the behaviour. A child who associates Christmas or parties as a time that starts off happy but often ends in disaster, may find it impossible to believe the experience will be any different at school. If a child is clearly showing that they are trying to destroy an event, it is useful to ask them to do a job in another class while the preparations are taking place. This can help to manage their anxieties and ensure they do not create a situation that results in them missing the event due to their behaviour. These children need to experience positive examples of events that they associate with negative outcomes to provide them with alternative evidence and experiences.

During the group work training I deliver, I encourage staff to think about the reason and the feeling behind the behaviour. When an adult is able to stop and think about the reason for the child's behaviour and what they may be feeling, instead of reacting instantly and making assumptions, they are beginning to put the child and their emotional needs first. By tentatively reflecting and commenting on what they are observing, the adult is providing a powerful message to the child about the validity of their feelings and opening up opportunities for exploring alternative ways of dealing with them. The group work programmes in this book provide a structured way for school staff to be able to integrate this into their way of working with children.

4 Integrating emotional well-being into the whole school

In the previous chapters I have discussed the importance of consistency in helping a child to develop emotionally and feel safe and secure at school. In order to be most effective, this consistent approach involves the whole school, is integrated into the curriculum and includes all staff, from lunchtime organisers to head teachers. A whole school approach to emotional health and well-being is a key component of achieving success for individual children within the school. When considering the emotional health and well-being approach that a school is going to use, it is essential for the head teacher to ensure it can be filtered easily across the school and embedded into the ethos.

Whole school approach

In order to identify the success of a school, it is useful to explore whether the children are happy, settled and achieving their full potential, along with identifying any barriers to being able to achieve this. Throughout their day at school children are expected to deal with a variety of challenges, such as trying new things, separating from their parent, etc. The way the school responds to the children's reactions to these events can influence their outcome. The school day is full of experiences that may evoke a range of different feelings in children and expose them to new and difficult situations. We may expect children to manage these without showing any response or reaction and may be surprised when they do. Children's fears need to be listened to and validated so they feel safe enough to voice them. School staff can develop self-awareness to ensure they are not being dismissive by using phrases such as, 'Don't be silly'. This can be discounting of the child's feelings and can exacerbate the child's fears.

The way that school staff respond to children showing their feelings has a big impact on their ability to understand and express them in a healthy way. It is important to consider how much the school accepts and encourages the expression of all feelings so children receive the message 'all feelings are okay', otherwise children may believe that it is not appropriate to show they feel sad, angry or cross. They may think that it is not acceptable to have or express painful feelings, only happy ones. Children need help with all their feelings from adults they can trust and feel safe with, so they are able to understand them and don't feel overwhelmed.

Table 4.1 Potential emotional impact of the school day

Situation	Feeling
Leave their parent	Scared
Follow rules	Overwhelmed
Listen to instructions	Confused
Manage changes such as having a new teacher	Terrified
Eat lunch in a large hall	Intimidated

The messages that children receive from the school environment and school staff can also reinforce how they view themselves and how they experience the world. These experiences can provide subtle messages about issues such as trust and responsibility through small everyday tasks. For example, if a child is given a job to do such as helping to tidy the book corner, they are given the messages 'I can trust you' and 'you can be responsible'.

Making assumptions

Schools have a commitment to assessing each child's literacy and numeracy levels and providing additional support through interventions such as booster groups for children who may need it. However, in terms of social and emotional development they do not assess a child's social skills but may sometimes reprimand them if they have difficulty in this area. We may expect children to be at a certain developmental level and make assessments based on their chronological rather than social and emotional age. For example, a 5-year-old who finds it difficult to share may be operating at an emotional level of a 3-year-old. It can be useful to consider the social and emotional skills that we may assume children have, as we may think they are able to share, listen, cooperate, sit quietly, sit still, and follow instructions. We can make assumptions that a child's age and developmental level are linked, but for some children there can be a big gap in this being a reality. It is crucial that children are not punished for their developmental difficulties, e.g. not being able to share, but instead are provided with opportunities to practise and develop those skills as they would be with other areas of their development. Does your school provide extra help and support in some areas, yet punish or reprimand children for not having the skills we expect them to have in others?

Staff strategy – visual reminders

If a child finds it difficult to share, take turns, etc. with other children, take photos of them doing this and create a book. Use it daily to remind them of the expected behaviour and how they have achieved it. For example, 'This is me sharing the Lego®', 'This is me waiting in the queue'.

This book can be used to reinforce the behaviour you would like them to do. For example, 'I remember when you were really good at sharing; let's have a look at that photo again.'

School staff may also presume that a child has a level of language and a cognitive understanding of the meaning of certain words. For some children, skills such as sitting still and listening are difficult to understand and even harder to put into practice. When children are operating at a much younger age in terms of their social and emotional development, they require extra support and clear explanations to enable them to achieve this. The group work programmes in this book can be used to enable children who need extra support to develop a range of age-appropriate behaviour.

Opportunities in the school day

Throughout the course of a school day there are many situations that may enable children to feel good about themselves and to achieve success. These opportunities may need to be adapted to enable every child to experience positive results, just as we are able to differentiate a child's learning to achieve this. There are also opportunities at school for children to experience disappointment and failure and for school staff to help them with the feelings these situations may evoke. This is an important aspect of developing resilience. The task of all adults in school is to acknowledge these feelings as they occur and help the child to manage them. It is important not to let a child win a game every time they play with an adult, as this is unrealistic and will not build resilience. It is far better to help the child understand that everyone wins and loses at times and to help them explore and express their feelings about this. This can help them to develop persistence, determination and motivation, rather than feeling overwhelmed and devastated. As discussed in previous chapters, this can be easier for some children to achieve due to their life experiences, and an individual needs-led approach can support this process.

Lunchtime

Lunchtimes in schools can be the most challenging part of the day, especially if the weather results in children having to be kept inside. The lunch period can be a difficult time for children as it is generally less structured and may feel disorganised and chaotic. This can be especially hard for children whose home lives may mirror this. The most effective way of managing this situation is to link a lunchtime organiser with each class who will ideally follow that class through the school, so there is some consistency of staff for the children. This can be difficult to implement, as the lunchtime staff team may change frequently as staff leave the school. However, the more that all school staff feel they are an essential part of the school, and have the opportunity to have their thoughts and feelings listened to, the more likely they are to continue working at the school. It is essential that all staff feel valued and appreciated in their role, including the lunchtime staff. In some schools, the lunchtime organisers may be involved in other roles around the school, such as listening to children read. This enables them to feel more integrated into the school and they are also more familiar to the children. This is particularly useful for the Foundation Stage children and can help them feel more settled at lunchtime, which can be a difficult time for children that struggle with change and lack of structure.

The lunchtime staff also need opportunities to develop skills and expertise and to be provided with guidance and support. Therefore, it can be beneficial to enable them to attend staff training on emotional well-being to ensure a consistent approach across the school. Staff can often focus on telling children what they do not want them to do, rather than making it clear what they should be doing. Instead, try replacing 'don't' with 'do' and see if it makes a difference.

Staff strategy for lunchtime organisers

As a staff team, work in pairs and compile a list of examples of behaviour that you may ask children not to do, e.g. 'Don't push when you are in the dinner queue'. Change each example into the behaviour you would like to see.

Don't say	Do say
Don't push when you are in the dinner queue.	Thank you for lining up nicely.

Compile a list of the behaviour you would like to see and ensure you all use it each day to provide consistency across the school. Meet with the team again and review whether you have noticed a difference in the children's behaviour.

Managing changes in the school day

As mentioned in previous chapters, the experience of consistency and predictability is essential for children's emotional well-being. Class teachers can contribute to this by acknowledging any changes throughout the day; for example, ensuring their class are made aware of when they are having their preparation time during the week. This can be helped further if the teacher returns to class afterwards to say 'goodbye' to the children at the end of the day. This may result in the class being able to manage their teacher's absence more easily and improved behaviour knowing they will be returning at the end of the day to check on the class and review the afternoon. A visual plan of the day can be helpful so that it can be referred to regularly and events crossed off it so children can see the end of the day approaching. This is particularly important for young children and those with separation issues, as they may have no sense of whether or when their parent is returning. Frequent references to this visual plan can be made throughout the day and used by other people who are providing cover for staff to ensure consistency. It is also possible for schools to use a similar approach when they are employing a supply teacher for the day. For example, the class teacher could leave a note to be read to the class at the start of the day. This would enable the class to manage their feelings more easily and provide a sense of predictability for them.

> Dear Class,
> Remember that I am on a course today to learn more exciting ways that I can help you with your reading. I will be back in class tomorrow morning and look forward to seeing you all then. I hope you all have a good day and show your supply teacher what a great class you are.
> Mrs Omoboye

In order to ensure there is a consistent approach to behaviour and class expectations, any supply staff that are covering staff absences can also be provided with guidelines of how to manage behaviour. A supply teacher who manages behaviour by intimidating children or shouting can undo the ethos the school is trying to create. For example, 'In this school we encourage positive behaviour by acknowledging and praising the behaviour we would like to see increasing and find it helps the children if all staff use a calm, clear voice rather than shouting.'

Transition

Some children find any change extremely difficult, as it can evoke feelings of loss, anxiety and uncertainty. It is useful, therefore, that children's transitions to new classes are managed with patience and understanding. For a child who has experienced many changes and uncertainty in their life outside school, the transition to a new class and new teacher can be overwhelming. Children have to adapt to a new relationship, maybe a different way of working and a new classroom environment, all at the end of spending six weeks away from school. The move from nursery to Reception and from Reception to Year 1 is enormous for young children and can create many anxieties. It is beneficial if children are given plenty of notice about this and if there can be several visits to their new class and opportunities to spend time with their new teacher. The more time that can be allocated to this before the summer holiday, the easier the transition and settling-in process will be on their return to/starting school.

Staff strategy – helping with transition

Teachers who will be having the class after the summer break can send each child a card over the holiday acknowledging they are looking forward to seeing them back at school and having them in their class.

I suggested the above activity to some Foundation staff a few years ago, and although it can feel like yet another thing to do at the end of the school year, they have all found it makes an enormous difference in helping the children to remember them and adjust to being back. The staff are now committed to doing it each year. Many of the children make reference to it and it can help the parents to keep the memory of school alive for them during the long break.

The first few weeks of term can be very challenging for children and staff and an important time to focus on developing and building the new relationship. Focusing on relationships enables them to feel safe and to relax and engage with their learning. If this is not prioritised, it can be very difficult to retrace and rebuild this. It is important that this is a gradual process and that allowances are made for children who may have difficulty building a new relationship.

Staff strategy – developing a connection

Provide an opportunity for each child to make a picture of their favourite person or toy and go round the class ensuring you talk to each child individually. This can be a good way of making an initial connection with each child in a relaxed way. As the focus is on the picture, it can help children who find new relationships frightening and overwhelming. They can also be referred to later in the year if there appear to be difficulties building a relationship with particular children.

The role of school staff

A beneficial tool for all school staff is the ability to reflect on themselves and their practice in an honest and open manner and consider how it may feel to be a child in their school. In order for them to do this, they need to feel safe and reassured that their observations will be heard and responded to in a supportive way. This can start with the head teacher and other senior members of staff and filter down the school to the lunchtime organisers and office staff. The relationships and professionalism between staff across the school can create either a supportive and effective team or a divided group of people who are all struggling to go to work every day.

Qualities to develop in all staff

- Are all staff approachable?
- Are they supportive of each other?
- Can they rely on each other?
- Do they work as a team or compete against each other?
- Are they open and receptive to change?
- Are they honest about themselves and their work?

- Do they maintain professionalism and confidentiality?
- Are they able to reflect and admit their mistakes?
- Are they motivated and committed to the children and the school?
- Do they model good working practice?
- Are they resilient?

Staff training

The experience of high-quality, inspirational training is of paramount importance for all staff in school, and opportunities to access additional training relevant to their role need to be available to all staff. The impact of this experience can be filtered across the school and new ideas and initiatives may be met with excitement and enthusiasm. Staff can be supported with identifying relevant training by formal and informal discussions and feedback on their performance. I feel it is beneficial to give feedback to staff on their relationships with children, not just their performance during lesson observations, as this is such a crucial aspect of their role in school. The relationships between children and staff are discussed in more detail in Chapter 5.

Staff relationships

The quality of the relationships between staff in school impacts on their ability to work together effectively and to model positive relationships to the children. The relationship between the class teacher, teaching assistant and support workers in their class need to be harmonious to ensure they are able to work together effectively. The relationship between staff working in the same class needs to incorporate open and honest communication along with mutual respect and appreciation. This can be demonstrated in front of the children so they are able to experience the impact of relating to other people in this way. When children have experienced living with disharmony and conflict, they are more receptive to noticing this in other relationships.

If the relationship between staff is one of mistrust, resentment and animosity, then this may be witnessed by the children through verbal and non-verbal interactions. When a child feels there is conflict between staff they may become aware of this and feel anxious, rather than engaging with their learning. Some children are very tuned in to relationships and will recognise atmospheres and behaviours between staff that can make them worried and anxious. Children need school to be a haven where they feel safe and protected, and any negative feelings between staff and a difficult atmosphere will prevent this from happening. There are opportunities to show children how to manage feelings and conflict between people through the relationships between all staff across the school.

Staff morale

Adults working in school need to feel valued and supported in their work in order to be productive, and the morale of the staff can impact on the children in a positive or negative way. All adults working in school have a responsibility to create a happy and relaxed atmosphere for children, or to decide what they can do to change it. Working in schools can be a demanding and exhausting but rewarding and enjoyable job. In order for staff to work most effectively and give their best to the children, they need to feel happy, supported and fulfilled. It is important they feel they are making a difference and that they are an essential cog in the wheel of school life. The school needs to be emotionally safe for staff in order to be emotionally safe for children.

Supporting each other

When school staff are confronted with challenging and disruptive behaviour from children, it can be difficult to remain calm, to stay focused on the child and not to feel upset and angry. There may be pressure to demonstrate they are able to manage the child's behaviour either by the expectations they put on themselves or real and imagined expectations from other members of staff. It is essential that staff support and encourage each other with this in order that the person dealing with the behaviour doesn't feel helpless and inadequate. When children feel hurt and upset and are unable to deal with their feelings, they may target the person they are close to and feel safe with, such as a teaching assistant or support worker. If this happens, it is essential that staff feel they have support and guidance from other members of staff, along with space and time to think about the child and their needs. This can enable them to develop resilience, so they are able to reflect on the situation without taking things personally and react appropriately in the best interests of the child.

Appropriate staff behaviour

As mentioned previously, the messages we are communicating to children as adults have a significant impact on them. When working in schools, it is necessary for staff to have an awareness of how their behaviour may influence the children on a daily basis. Staff whose behaviour is loud and outgoing may unnerve and intimidate children who may easily experience adults as frightening and overwhelming. If staff constantly joke and laugh with children, it is important to check that they understand when you are being serious. It is our job as adults to decide and implement the boundaries around this for children, and not to reprimand them if they become over excited. Some children are overly aware of what adults are saying and doing and may look for hidden clues in people's behaviour. For example, Rosie, aged 5, noticed her teacher was quiet and offered to help tidy up, asking, 'Are you sad?'

Reflect: How do I behave?

- Are my interactions always appropriate?
- What are my tone of voice and facial expression communicating?
- Do I have consistent boundaries, no matter how I am feeling?

All children react differently to shouting, and while this may get their attention immediately in some situations, it can also provide mixed messages to children. If we reprimand children for shouting or ask them to speak nicely to each other and then children hear staff shouting, we are causing confusion. We are saying one behaviour is acceptable for adults but not for children. There are occasions when it may be necessary for an adult to raise their voice in school; for example, if a child is about to fall or hurt themselves. However, adults may use shouting as a way of trying to manage children's behaviour. For a child who has experienced domestic violence or lives in a family where shouting is used as a way of communicating, this can be a very frightening experience. The child may tune out and appear to not be listening but actually may be feeling scared and unsure what to do. This can create even more anxiety and stress for the child.

Managing feelings

The school setting provides an ideal situation to demonstrate how to express and manage feelings on a daily basis. Staff can model ways of expressing their own feelings, often without being aware of it. Staff who sulk or moan, or patronise and humiliate other members of staff, parents and children, are providing powerful messages about how to manage feelings. If schools have clear expectations about children's behaviour and what is acceptable and unacceptable, they need to ensure this is implemented at all times by all staff. It is essential that schools provide a consistent message to everyone in school and are not contradictory in their approach.

The way that the school staff react to everyday situations provides an opportunity to model ways of dealing with feelings to children. For example, if a member of staff makes a mistake or breaks something, this can be used as an opportunity to acknowledge that this happens to everyone and that it is an important part of life. It can offer the chance to explain that mistakes allow us to learn and try things, rather than covering it up so children may think that adults never make mistakes. Throughout the school day there are so many learning opportunities that are not part of the curriculum that can be used for children to learn invaluable life lessons. For example, do adults apologise to children, do they demonstrate the behaviour we want children to have? Do children feel that there is room for them to make mistakes and that they get praise for being brave and trying things?

As adults, we all have a responsibility to help children to understand and express their feelings, rather than feel scared or overwhelmed by them. There are endless opportunities for school staff to share their experiences of managing their own feelings throughout the day. If there is a commitment from all school staff to use emotional vocabulary and share experiences appropriately with children, this can result in children being able to mirror this behaviour. This can be achieved by acknowledging situations as they arise throughout the day; for example, 'When I try something new, I can get a sick feeling in my stomach. I know that this is because it can feel scary doing something for the first time.' Making statements such as, 'Everyone has difficult feelings sometimes and it can help to tell people when we feel like this', can contribute to children's awareness of themselves and other people.

Using reflective language

We can also provide positive messages to children in a subtle way throughout the school day by thinking about and commenting on what is happening by using reflective language to tentatively explore what a child may be experiencing. This has been discussed in more detail in Chapter 3.

Table 4.2 Impact of positive reflective responses

Reflective response	Message to child
I've been thinking about how hard it is for you to sit on the carpet	You are worth thinking about
I'm going to ask Mrs Jones to spend some time with you and teach you how to put your coat on; I can see it frustrates you when you try to do it	You are worth helping
It's important that everyone has a turn at being at the front of the line	Your needs matter
You looked sad when you didn't get chosen for the dance session. I wonder if you'd like to choose a friend and help me unpack the new books	You are important

The examples of reflective language provided enable it to be integrated into the school day. For example, if a child is struggling or finding a task difficult, it can help to reflect, 'It can be difficult when we get things wrong', or, 'It can feel frustrating when we are trying to do something and we can't work out how to do it.' This enables the child to feel noticed and understood, along with helping them to identify what frustration feels like. Over time, this enables the child to link the feelings with the word and to make that connection themselves. This may result in them being able to use the word themselves when they next have that feeling. It assists enormously if school staff are able to use this as a way of commenting on their own feelings; for example, 'I felt sad when I was unwell and missed the school trip.' See Chapters 11 and 12 for more examples of using reflective language.

Using affirmative language

The use of language is an important aspect of the behavioural approach within school, and using affirmative language that focuses on the behaviour you want to see, rather than the behaviour you don't, is a beneficial approach. For example, 'Please walk to the hall' rather than 'Don't run!' will often be more effective. When we focus on the aspects of behaviour we don't want, then that is what we will see. Children just hear the word 'run' and it gives them an idea, in the same way as we may say to a toddler, 'Don't touch the plug!', they just hear the word plug and immediately head towards it.

This approach is useful for children who have poor self-regulation and impulse control and may find it extremely difficult to change their behaviour and not do things. For example, if at home a child has to interrupt other people and talk over them to be heard, then it can be difficult not to act in the same way at school. A gentle reminder such as, 'Remember, we all need to listen to each other', can help to remind them of the behavioural expectation.

Listening to children

It is useful to consider how much time is allocated to listening to children's thoughts, feelings and ideas during the school day, and explore whether children feel safe enough to do this. It is beneficial to provide opportunities for children to do this throughout the school year and for their ideas to be acknowledged and responded to in a positive and accepting manner. All children need regular opportunities to make choices, along with validation that their ideas and feelings matter and are important.

Integrating emotional vocabulary into the curriculum

During the school day children may be asked to experience situations that adults may not feel comfortable experiencing, such as being vulnerable and sharing things about themselves that adults may find difficult to do. In class, an adult may randomly choose a child to answer a question, thereby exposing them in a way we would be uncomfortable as adults. How many of us have attended training where we would feel uncomfortable if the facilitator randomly singled us out to participate?

Reflect: Would this feel comfortable?

- What do we ask children to do?
- How may it feel for them?
- How would I feel if someone asked me to do this?
- How can we change this to make it feel easier and less intimidating for children?

There are many opportunities during the school day to introduce and familiarise children with emotional vocabulary. It is essential to use this as often as possible so it becomes a recognised way of interacting and avoids children being asked to do something without naming and explaining it. For example, if a child hits another child and is asked why they behaved in this way, it is not realistic to expect them to explain if they are not provided with the appropriate vocabulary to be able to do this. The school staff ensuring they use regular opportunities to introduce emotional vocabulary to children can assist them with this.

Choices and responsibility

In school, children are provided with opportunities to learn about making choices and can begin to understand some of the basic concepts of taking responsibility. This has a positive impact on their confidence, self-esteem and self-worth. If children are given choices over small things throughout the day, such as choosing to play outside or with a specific activity, this can help them to understand more easily about the consequences of other choices they may make, such as choosing to hit someone has a consequence of missing out on playtime.

When we give a child a choice we are saying:

- I trust you.
- Your views are important.
- Your needs matter.

Creating the right environment

The physical environment that is created in a school impacts on the emotional well-being of everyone who comes in to school. For children who experience disorganisation and unpredictability outside school, the organised and ordered environment of school contributes to their sense of safety and well-being. Classrooms that are clean, tidy and enable children to find things easily and have things in the same place so children can access them easily, provide a sense of stability in children's otherwise unstable lives. A child who returns to school after a chaotic and unstructured weekend can feel soothed by knowing the Lego® will be in the same place on Monday morning. The children can be encouraged to have responsibility for taking care of their class, and this can involve a teamwork approach. A sense of ownership and pride can be encouraged across the school, but specifically in relation to individual classes. It is important to involve children in this as it is their space, and the more comfortable they feel the easier they will find it to engage with their learning.

Feeling safe and secure at school

School staff may make assumptions and have their own ideas about children's understanding of safety, but it is important to clarify this with them. The staff can also lead by example through their own behaviour and by ensuring that clear explanations are offered to children. For example, if a child is running while holding a pair of scissors, they need an example of the alternative behaviour you would like to see, along with an explanation of why they need to change their behaviour, such as, 'Please walk when you are carrying scissors, because if you trip or fall you could hurt yourself, and I don't want that to happen.' It is important to be aware of not making assumptions about children's understanding or awareness of safety because of their age. Some children have no sense of danger because they may never have been made aware of it. These children may look confused when explanations about safety are offered to them. Acknowledging that you don't want a child to hurt themselves or that you want to keep them safe may come as a surprise for some children who may be physically or emotionally hurt by adults outside school.

Staff strategy – increasing awareness of safety

Take small groups of children for a safety walk around the class, both inside and out, and ask them to identify the dangers both inside and in the playground. This enables you to assess each child's awareness and understanding of safety. It may bring you some surprises.

Emotional safety

Schools can play an important role in promoting children's awareness of emotional safety by exploring how we behave towards other people and why. It is beneficial to discuss why we are kind and care for each other and identify the feelings this may evoke. Children need to trust that the adults in school will protect them from harm in order to feel emotionally safe at school. This can be achieved by a clear and consistent policy for dealing with bullying and ensuring it is implemented by all staff. Schooldays can be the best or worst days of our lives, and some of this is affected by friendships and peer relationships. It is essential that all children across school understand that any form of bullying is not acceptable and that staff understand that children who bully need urgent help. This is discussed in more detail in Chapter 3 and Chapter 5.

It can be useful to consider how your school responds to children who are late arriving at school. If a child is late to a primary school then it is not their fault, although some parents may try and convince you that it is. For a child who is late, the embarrassment and shame of having to walk into their class when the lesson has already started is enough for them to have to deal with. Imagine how we, as adults, feel if we are late for training or a conference and have to walk into a room; now consider how difficult this can be for children to manage, especially if it happens on a regular basis.

Case study

Kyle, aged 4, arrives ten minutes late for school. He looks tired, anxious and dishevelled. There is a history of domestic violence in his family and his mum is finding it hard to cope with his three younger siblings.

Teacher A response:
'Oh, you're late again. Tuck your shirt in.'

Teacher B response:
'Morning, Kyle. It's nice to see you. I can see you look tired; are you okay?'

The response of Teacher B is far more likely to encourage and enable the child to settle and engage with their learning than the response of Teacher A, which is likely to increase their levels of anxiety and stress. The teacher who responds to a child's lateness by trying to make the child feel welcome and part of the class, however frustrating it may be, will help the child to feel reassured and valued.

An environment where children feel safe enough to make mistakes and are supported to learn from them provides an excellent learning opportunity. However, if a child who accidentally breaks something is reprimanded and punished, they may not only be too scared to admit it when they do this in the future, thinking 'It is not okay to make mistakes', rather it may also prevent them from trying in the future and evoke a sense of shame about their behaviour. If an adult responds with compassion rather than irritation, a child learns that making mistakes and breaking things is a part of life.

Behaviour system

The school behaviour system provides the foundations of the school and is most effective when it is implemented consistently across the school in terms of expectations and responses to behaviour. Any inconsistencies between adults may make children feel scared and anxious, resulting in them being quiet and withdrawn or challenging and controlling. This requires a commitment from all staff and an understanding of the importance of this. The behaviour system needs to be clear and understandable by children across the school, and the behavioural expectations for the school need to be realistic and achievable by all the children to enable everyone to achieve success. It is useful to ask the children for feedback on their understanding of it and how it works to ensure it has been understood. For example, if a child is regularly having difficulty following a particular rule, encourage the class teacher or another adult in school to check their understanding of it.

Helping children to understand behavioural expectations

It is important not to make assumptions about a child's understanding of behaviour without assessing it, just as we would assess their literacy or numeracy. For example, if a school rule is, 'We are kind and gentle with each other', it is important to give the children examples of how they can achieve this. Some of the expectations we have about children's behaviour in school may make it very difficult for them to achieve success. For example, during carpet time children may be expected to sit on a sometimes cold, hard floor and are reprimanded for being unable to do this without fidgeting or moving about. Most adults would find this difficult, yet we expect children to manage it. There may be limited alternatives, as there may not be enough chairs for children, but if staff can acknowledge that it's a difficult thing to do, they are at least validating the children's experience.

To create an effective school environment, the following attributes are useful:

Table 4.3 Useful attributes

Staff need	Children need
Patience	Understanding
Encouragement	Nurturing
Motivation	Consistency
Determination	Support
Support	Praise
Commitment	Encouragement
Tolerance	Recognition

It is essential in schools that school staff attempt to explore why children are behaving in particular ways, what they may be trying to communicate, how they feel and what can be done to help them with this. The more that children can feel understood and supported in trying to change their behaviour, the increased likelihood there is that this will happen. Imagine, as adults, if no one ever tried to understand us or help us to make changes: how would that feel?

Using behaviour charts

Behaviour charts are an invaluable way of monitoring children's behaviour and providing them with targets to achieve. However, they are most effective when they enable children to achieve some degree of success and to see the immediate results of their efforts. It is unrealistic to give a child more than one target. In the same way as we would not expect an adult to stop smoking, take up running, go on a diet and stop drinking all at the same time, because it would be unrealistic to expect them to achieve and maintain all this. We need to apply the same philosophy when setting targets for children. For example, an initial target of 'good listening' for a child can be extended to develop additional changes once the child has experienced success. It is essential to ensure that the child has a clear understanding of what the target means, i.e. what 'good listening' means, to ensure they are able to achieve success.

Involving parents

Parents play a vital role in the school, and for a child to reach their full potential it is essential that they are as involved as possible, have positive experiences of the school and feel valued and supported in their role. It is most effective for the child if the relationship between parents and school is a harmonious one. It is worthwhile making parents aware of and explaining any interventions that are being offered in school so they are able to use a similar approach with their child at home. For example, a parent whose child was involved in the group work friendship programme was able to support this work by encouraging the child to practise the skills at home alongside the group, therefore maximising the potential for change occurring. As the parents in the school became more aware of the group work programmes and their effectiveness, this resulted in increased numbers asking for their children to participate. See Part Two for more information on the group work programme.

Developing life skills

The school setting is the ideal place for children to learn about and practise developing essential life skills, and the opportunity to do this can be integrated into the school curriculum through lessons and activities. The possibilities to do this are enormous and enable staff to be creative in their approach, along with providing a template for developing and managing relationships. Qualities such as honesty, tolerance, compassion, courage, patience, etc. can all be integrated into the curriculum and develop resilience and other skills. It is important not to make assumptions about the skills that a child may have as this will depend on their external experiences, as discussed in more detail in Chapter 2. The group work programmes in this book provide an important part of an effective whole school approach by creating opportunities for children to have additional support with emotional and social skills, along with validating and appreciating their individuality.

For the group work programmes to be most effective, they need to be part of a whole school approach that reinforces the skills and experiences for children and staff. For example, Marcus, aged 4, found it difficult to make friends and could be bossy and controlling towards other children. In the group work sessions he tried to keep hold of the pot of pens at the start of each session and reluctantly handed them over when the facilitator explored the possibility of sharing them with the other child. The facilitator met weekly with Marcus's class teacher and the teaching assistant in his class, sharing the skills they had been practising in the session and encouraging them to help him practise these in class. This approach enabled them to encourage him to transfer these skills outside the sessions and provide the additional support he needed. This resulted in his friendships and confidence and self-esteem improving as he felt better about himself. If the group facilitator can liaise regularly with the parents, head teacher, class teacher and other adults working with the children across the school to provide feedback on the child's behaviour and share information, then this enables it to be fully integrated across the school rather than seen as a token gesture that may be hard to sustain.

5 Developing positive and meaningful relationships at school

Early relational experiences

In order for children to be able to build relationships with other people, it is necessary for them to have a template of how to do this. A child's first relationship is with their main caregiver, and this is usually a mother, father, grandparent or other relative. The quality of this primary relationship can determine the standard of future relationships, as children will often approach new relationships based on their previous experiences. Children who have experienced their first relationship with a parent or carer that is nurturing, supportive, consistent and loving are able to develop an internal feeling of safety and security. This experience enables the child to explore freely and have a natural curiosity and excitement about life. As their early needs for food and stimulation have been responded to and their early interactions through babbling and gurgling have been met with enthusiasm and delight, they learn that their needs are recognised and met and they are worth thinking about and caring for, resulting in high self-esteem. They may present in school as having the skills and ability to build and maintain relationships and respond positively to help and support with this when needed.

However, a child who has had an erratic, inconsistent and unpredictable experience of early relationships may find it more difficult to internalise a sense of safety and security and may experience relationships as frightening and unreliable. If a parent or carer is emotionally or physically unavailable to the child, perhaps rejecting their needs and ignoring them or pushing them away when they cry, the child learns that their needs are not worthwhile and that if you seek comfort from someone you may be rejected. They may present in school as being quiet, withdrawn and self-contained. 'He seems happy on his own' may be how this child is referred to. For these children, relationships are frightening and to be avoided wherever possible, even if it means missing out on positive experiences. Some children who have experienced neglect or abuse may find it difficult to approach staff or allow them to comfort them when they are distressed or upset. These children may have developed self-reliance as a way of coping with this and can find the transition to starting nursery more difficult. This can impact on their social relationships with the other children as they may feel less emotionally and physically safe; these children can benefit greatly from being involved in the group work programmes.

Children need to have positive experiences of separating from their main carer to be able to manage the school day and relationships that occur within the school setting with both adults and children. If a child has not had this positive experience, it is possible to repair some of this by providing consistent, predictable, positive nurturing relationships in school with school staff. This experience can transform a child's early relational experiences and provide them with a strong base from which to develop and grow. Children also need opportunities for fun, laughter and playfulness, which can help to develop and strengthen their relational experiences.

Case study

Mohammed, aged 3, finds it difficult to settle in nursery and can be restless and disruptive at various times throughout the day. He also finds it hard to sit still and follow the adult's instructions.

Possible reasons for his behaviour:

- His mum was hospitalised for several months after a car crash when he was three months old and he was looked after by several family members during this time.
- His mum then experienced long periods of depression and was often unable to look after him properly.

The school understands that Mohammed needs some help to manage his behaviour in class and has made the teaching assistant available for him to access for extra relational support for 15 minutes at the start of each day. This involves play activities, such as blowing bubbles, rolling a ball to each other and playing catch in a small room off the nursery. Mohammed enjoys these sessions and is responding well to instructions, gradually making more eye contact, and is now familiar with this being part of his routine. This experience provides him with an alternative experience to the one he had with his mum and enables him to practise and develop social and emotional skills in a small and safe environment. When we are able to provide opportunities to fill relational gaps for children, they have more capacity for learning.

Being a parent can be extremely stressful and challenging at times, and some parents may have little or no experience of receiving positive parenting themselves. A parent or caregiver who is overwhelmed by their own needs or difficulties may find it hard to respond to their child's needs in a consistent and caring way. They may be trying to keep themselves physically and emotionally safe, for example, if they are experiencing domestic violence, and may be unable to meet the needs of their child. Children who have this early experience may respond by being clingy, watchful and mistrusting of people. They may present in school as being controlling and manipulative in order to manage their high levels of anxiety. They may often feel very scared but have learned to hide this through aggressive behaviour towards other children and school staff. They may focus on objects rather than people, as they are easier to predict and manage; for example, a child who always fiddles with bits of paper or seems to have an endless supply of items in their pocket, or puts things in their mouth. This child may need to have these in order to feel safe, secure and settled in school. It is important for staff working in schools to consider this when removing objects that may appear to be rubbish or to have no significance, as they may be of crucial importance and represent security for the child.

Staff strategy – helping children to manage their anxiety

Give the child an object, such as a plastic animal or finger puppet, and explain this is for them to have with them if they need help to do their work or sit still. Explain that they can choose a name for it and it has to stay in school so they can make a bed for it in their tray or drawer if they would like to.

The above strategy has been successfully implemented in many schools, and although there is often initial uncertainty from school staff about the child just playing with it and not concentrating, it has been proven that the opposite is true. Having an object to hold at times during the day has helped to reduce the child's anxiety and therefore enabled them to concentrate and focus on their learning more easily. In a school I work in I suggested this for a child in nursery and he was given a finger puppet to look after. He made a box for it and started putting pretend food from the home corner in the box for it, explaining to his teacher that the puppet was hungry. This provided an ideal opportunity for him to learn about nurturing and taking care of things.

Relational experiences within the family

The ideas discussed in Chapter 2, which explores the impact of the family on the child's ability to learn and succeed at school, examine in more detail the effect of these experiences on children. If a child's needs are considered and met consistently during childhood, they have a different experience from a child who has not had this. If a child feels unconditionally loved and valued for who they are and the joy they bring to their parents/carers, it is easier for them to approach and cope with school life. If a child feels that they are loved conditionally depending on their behaviour or not at all because of their behaviour, their sense of being worthwhile, valued and bringing joy to other people may be an unfamiliar concept to them. As discussed previously, children initially develop core beliefs and ideas about themselves within the family, and these are validated by the messages they receive about themselves.

Table 5.1 Development of core beliefs within the family

Core belief	Validated by
I'm not good enough	Frequent criticism
My needs don't matter	Parents' needs always coming first
I'm not safe	Unpredictable and inconsistent parenting
I'm a bad person	Experiencing abuse/domestic violence

Some families may find it difficult to model positive relationships with each other or with people outside the family. As the family is the child's first classroom, the concepts they learn and experiences of how relationships are made and sustained are of crucial importance. This can be a major conflict between home and school. When a child learns within the family that relationships are about power, control and manipulation, and are encouraged to fight verbally and physically to get their needs met, the school setting, with its different set of relational expectations and rules, can be a very confusing place.

When a child experiences their parents regularly arguing or fighting, they may think it is their fault, that they are responsible and that somehow they need to try and do something to make it better. They may become preoccupied with this and have little or no time or space to engage with their learning or to develop friendships. Sometimes a child is constantly trying to repair their parents' relationship by their behaviour; for example, 'If I put all my toys away, then Mum will be happy and won't shout at Dad when he comes home from the pub and tell him to move out.' This may result in them appearing uninterested at school as they are thinking of new ways to make things better at home. This can also occur for children who may have a parent who is depressed, and although they are physically present may be 'emotionally absent' and find it hard to interact or engage with their child. This behaviour may serve as a self-fulfilling prophecy for their internal script that is already telling them they are wrong and bad and things are their fault. This experience may manifest itself in the child learning to please other people all the time, and therefore it is crucial that they have experiences that confirm their needs do matter and are important.

It is a challenge to encourage children to develop and implement the school's relationship system in a way that is not demonising or criticising the child's experience within their family. How do we manage this without giving the message that school is right and your family is wrong?

Case study

Malakai, aged 5, witnessed his mum and dad hitting each other whenever they were angry, which was frequently. He learned and witnessed repeatedly that this is how to respond to conflict. The messages he received were that if someone says or does something that you do not like, then you need to hit them. This was reinforced by his parents telling him he was soft if he didn't demonstrate this behaviour towards other children in the street.

At school, Malakai was very confused. If he behaved in a way that his parents approved of and that pleased them, then he received disapproval and got in trouble at school. He was constantly having to juggle two conflicting ways of behaving and would just be getting used to this when there was a school holiday and he would have to start all over again.

Relational templates

The relationships that are demonstrated between the adults within the child's family provide powerful experiences of how to manage these outside it. While children may not be able differentiate between helpful and harmful responses to situations, they are reliant on adults to provide examples of this for them. The way that this is shown to children can either help or hinder their ability to build relationships themselves.

Reflect: What messages may be provided by the following situation?

A child witnesses their parents arguing and fighting. Mum tells Dad to leave and Mum gets a new boyfriend. Mum tries to stop Dad seeing the child as a way of punishing him. Dad refuses to give Mum any money until she lets him see the child and tries to phone the child to speak to them. Mum refuses to let the child speak to Dad or have any contact with him.

Messages to the child:

- Conflicts are not resolvable.
- Relationships are replaceable (Mum gets new boyfriend).
- Relationships are about power and control.
- Relationships are not about compromise or negotiation.
- Relationships are confusing and unpredictable.
- My thoughts and feelings don't matter.

Children bring their templates of how to build and maintain relationships with them into school. Each child already has countless examples of relationships they have experienced and witnessed by the time they come to school, and their experiences at school can either reaffirm or challenge these.

Negative messages children may learn about relationships within the family:

- You have to fight for everything.
- Relationships are hard.
- Don't trust anyone.
- Everyone is out to get you.
- It's good to get one over on people.
- Having feelings is a weakness.
- It's good to hurt other people.
- Don't be vulnerable.

Within the family there are expectations that parents love each other and their children, but this can be difficult to do if a parent has not had this experience themselves and does not understand how to do this. The experience of how sibling relationships are established and managed within the family provides a useful opportunity for families to encourage children to practise and develop skills that will be beneficial at school and in the wider community. When children have had positive experiences of managing feelings of jealousy with siblings, along with dealing with conflict and competition in a positive way, this enables them to transfer these skills to experiences at school. The relational patterns that children are exposed to are internalised and may become a reality in school. Children develop their own internal guide to making friends and engaging in relationships with adults in school and this may manifest itself in their behaviour towards other people.

Table 5.2 What has this child been taught in their family?

Kindness	or	Aggression
Compassion		Humiliation
Respect		Degradation
Understanding		Hostility
Tolerance		Indifference
Acceptance		Rejection

Helping children to develop appropriate friendships

When children have had difficult experiences, it is important that the school recognises that they may not have the social and emotional skills appropriate for their age. It is vital that each child is assessed for this, rather than expecting them to automatically be able to manage relationships with children and school staff. It is crucial that we support children who do not have the skills to build and maintain friendships, rather than punish them for not having them. For example, to develop empathy it is necessary to be able to understand and make sense of the behaviour of another person; therefore, if children have not had the experience of this for themselves, they may find it difficult to have empathy towards other people and to understand their feelings. This can be demonstrated by children who appear to show no remorse or understand the impact of their behaviour when they have hurt someone, although it is also important to consider the child's developmental level and cognitive understanding.

The school setting provides the ideal situation for children to learn basic friendships skills and it is useful to explore opportunities within the school day to do this. Children who have friends feel happy, confident and good about themselves. They are more able to focus and engage with their learning, rather than feeling worried and anxious about their lack of friends and how they feel about themselves. The school can support children who need additional help to build friendship skills by using a caring approach that is nurturing rather than punitive, which will achieve more positive results.

The group work programmes provide an opportunity for children to receive additional support with their social and emotional development and enables them to develop the necessary skills to manage relationships more successfully. The activities and tasks are devised to enable children to practise social skills, such as sharing, compromising, negotiating, waiting for their turn, etc. – skills that some children may not have had the opportunity to develop outside school. The supportive environment created by the group facilitator enables children to experiment with behaving differently and taking a risk. For children who have no resilience, lack confidence and self-esteem, and can't manage their peer relationships, the chance to practise these skills in a safe and supportive environment can help eliminate their feelings of vulnerability and isolation. The group can encourage children to have good feelings about themselves by providing messages such as, 'You can contribute your ideas and do things well; people like you', which are all essential ingredients to enable children to build and sustain friendships. The sense of belonging created by being in the group on a weekly basis enables children to build an alliance with the other child group and assists them in building a friendship that may be transferred outside the group.

The activities and tasks in the group work programmes enable children to develop positive feelings about themselves through their behaviour. For example, an activity that involves making something for someone else (Week 5, Friendship programme) provides an opportunity to explore how this feels and why. This develops positive feelings and increases the likelihood of the behaviour being repeated outside the group so children activate those feelings about themselves again. For children who find the idea of sharing and giving something to someone else hard to do, the experience of being with one other child, along with the support and encouragement from the facilitator, can provide an opportunity for them to practise this. The development of these skills and the heightened awareness of other people enable friendship skills to be practised and implemented on a daily basis. For example, a child who was previously quiet and withdrawn may find his voice and start approaching the class teacher more often. The benefits of the group work programmes are discussed in more detail in Chapter 7.

Children who need help with friendships

There are a variety of reasons why some children find it more difficult to make friends and we have already explored some of these. When a child does not have the skills to make connections with other people, they may use their behaviour as a way of getting a response and being noticed; for example, a child who pokes or prods another child to make a connection because they do not have the language or social skills to know where to begin. For children who find making and keeping friends difficult, it can reinforce their sense of loneliness and isolation when they can't seem to get it right in making connections with other children.

Case study

Jermaine, aged 5, found it difficult to make friends with the other children in his class. He would hit them, push his way to the front of every line and snatch things if he wanted them.

Jermaine's poor social skills, emotional vulnerability and challenging behaviour all resulted in him behaving at the developmental level of a child of a much younger age. The other children were afraid of him and avoided being near him whenever possible, which reinforced to him that they didn't like him. This downward spiral can be difficult to break without additional help, nurture and support in school.

Staff strategy – kind hands chart

Talk to the child and explain and demonstrate how they can use their hands in a kind way. For example, picking something up for someone. Ensure they understand the difference between using their hands in a kind and unkind way. Make them a kind hands chart by dividing the day into small sections and giving them a sticker to put on their chart when they achieve this.

For children such as Jermaine, it may be difficult to understand the concept of being kind unless they are given concrete examples of the behaviours that we would like them to do. The use of a chart helps to focus on the behaviour that is expected of them and builds their confidence and self-esteem as they start to experience success. Even a small success should be celebrated with the child and parent, if possible. The responses from the other school staff and children can help to support this and enable the child to be viewed in a more positive way.

Reflect: Think of a child you know and consider the child's relational template

- What is this child's experience of relationships at home?
- What is this child's experience of relationships at school?
- What do they need?
- How can I help them with this?

Children who bully

Children who hit, hurt or try to control other children may be showing adults they desperately need help with their social and emotional skills. When a child displays any of these behaviours they are clearly communicating that they are unhappy and need help to feel better about themselves. Children who actively hurt others are often hurting themselves. Children who are happy and settled do not need to hurt other people.

Possible reasons for children bullying:

- low self-esteem;
- lack of confidence;
- negative sense of self, such as 'I'm a bad person, I'm not good enough';
- being bullied themselves;
- being controlled outside school so using control to feel powerful;
- lack of control and choices at home.

While it may be a challenge for school staff to look beyond the child's behaviour, this is the key to enabling them to change it. Children who display bullying behaviour need nurturing and to feel good about themselves.

Children who bully need:

- opportunities to develop personal strengths and qualities;
- to have choices and contribute to decision-making wherever possible;
- a positive relationship with an identified person who can get to know them and support them to get their needs met in more positive ways;
- school staff to show an interest in them and spend time getting to know them so they feel more positive about who they are.

Children who experienced multiple transitions

As mentioned in Chapter 2, children who have moved house and possibly moved school, too, may need extra support with friendships and adjusting to school life. They may require additional support settling in to the class and feeling comfortable at school. This can be achieved by providing additional adult help, if it is available, and preparing the class to welcome the newcomer. The experience of a new child starting in a class provides an ideal opportunity to work with the rest of the class to explore how this may feel and what they can do to help the child. It is a useful way to introduce concepts such as being kind, caring, thoughtful, etc. with the class and to enable them to practise and develop a new understanding and set of skills. The class teacher can consider who can be a friend to them and when and how this will be reviewed. If a new child is provided with a positive and welcoming start, this can help alleviate some anxieties the child may be feeling.

Consider your contribution

The vast majority of adults who choose to work in schools like working with children and enjoy their company. The key to any good relationship, including those between school staff and children, is the ability to self-reflect. This involves an honest appraisal of the following:

- What do I react to and why?
- What do I struggle with and why?
- What do I honestly think about children who show challenging behaviour and why?
- What do I honestly think about children who bully and why?
- What do I think about children who lie and why?
- What do I think about children who steal and why?
- What do I think about children who hit other children and adults and why?
- Am I as happy as I could be with the relationships I have with the children?
- If not, what could I do to change this?

The more honest that school staff can be with themselves about the behaviours and relationships that they find difficult and why, the more they are able to change this and improve the relationships they have with the children in their school. It may be a complex and painful task to do, but it can also be a liberating experience, resulting in staff ensuring they do not punish children for their behaviour because of how they are feeling. Some children may evoke difficult feelings in adults and school staff may start behaving differently towards them; for example, if a child has been rude to you it may be hard not to ignore them or be stricter with them the next time you see them.

It is essential that school staff look after and support each other's emotional well-being and are able to identify ways to manage their stress. Strategies such as going for a short walk around school, popping outside or having a cup of tea can all help to reduce the likelihood of stress levels increasing. School staff need to be able to look after and support themselves so they are able to look after and support the children. If staff are feeling fragile, stressed or vulnerable, this will impact on their ability to develop and maintain relationships with the children.

It is also useful if staff can separate the behaviour from the child and remember this is the way that the child is communicating – it is not a personal attack or a deliberate way of making your day more difficult. It is important that staff try and stay calm and model this for children and avoid getting into power struggles. If the adult is able to stay calm, this will help the child to regulate their own feelings. Explore what is motivating your response to a child and ensure you are responding in an adult way.

Table 5.3 Impact of adult's response on child's behaviour

Child's behaviour	Adult's response	Child's behaviour
Child is angry and shouting (child feels scared and anxious and thinks 'You can't manage me and I don't feel safe')	Adult feels angry and shouts back (adult feels scared and anxious and thinks 'I can't manage you')	Child increases level of anger and shouts louder (child feels terrified and thinks 'I knew you couldn't manage me')
Child is angry and shouting (child feels scared and anxious and thinks 'You can't manage me and I don't feel safe')	Adult responds with calm and reassuring tone of voice (adult feels in control and thinks 'I can manage you')	Child feels understood and soothed (child thinks 'I am beginning to feel safe again now')

If school staff are committed to having better relationships with children and are able to honestly reflect on the barriers that are preventing them from achieving this, then they have started on a journey to be able to achieve this. The following activity can be implemented using a class list every half term and is a useful way to keep evaluating your relationships with the children.

Reflect: How well do I know my class?

Look at your class list and consider the following:

- How well do I know the children in my class?
- How do I manage my relationships with quieter/shy/less confident children?
- Can I identify the children who find it hard to ask for help?
- Which children do I have good relationships with and why?

Staff experiences

Each member of school staff will have their own story and experience of their own schooling that they bring with them to work every day. This may have been a positive or negative event and may impact on their present-day experiences in school. It may affect the way they interact with the children, their beliefs about behaviour and how it should be responded to, along with how they feel about their job.

Reflect: How does your experience of school impact on your relationships with children and reactions to their behaviour?

Think of a child who you find challenging or difficult.

- What is it that you find difficult?
- Do they challenge you or ignore you?
- How does that make you feel?
- Why do you think they do this?
- What can you do to improve your relationship with that child?
- How would you feel if you achieved this?

Both school staff and children will bring experiences and ideas to the school setting each day. Children bring their own experiences of how behaviour is managed at home and in the wider community, along with attitudes to school and learning and an acceptable code of conduct they have learned. Adults have their own experiences of early childhood programming that they carry with them in to adulthood. School staff bring their own expectations about how behaviour should be managed, their own attitudes towards school and learning, along with an acceptable code of conduct they have learned. The more compatible these are, the increased likelihood of successful relational experiences occurring for staff and children.

The quality of the staff and child relationship

Reflect: On your journey into work each day, ask yourself:

- How do I feel?
- What am I bringing with me to school today?
- What can I do to ensure it doesn't have a negative impact on my relationships and my day?

The quality of the staff–child relationship affects the teacher both emotionally and professionally, and the child in terms of outcome, achievement and positive sense of self. The staff perception of the child affects the relationship between them and the staff's efforts to engage and motivate the child. There are some children that it is very easy for school staff to have a good relationship with. These children are often confident, articulate and pleasant to spend time with but who may also be quiet and eager to please. They are compliant and respond well to adult interactions and praise. However, it is the children that staff find most challenging and difficult to spend time with who need this time the most. These children may present as antagonistic, argumentative and disrespectful. They may appear to have no interest in building relationships with school staff and seem to go out of their way to make school life as hard as possible for themselves and everyone around them. It is not surprising, therefore, that most school staff would not choose to actively try and develop a relationship with them.

Staff strategy – challenge yourself

If there is a child in your class who you find particularly difficult or hard to connect with, set yourself the task of thinking of three positive things about them on your journey to work and spending five minutes with that child each day. Do this for a week and reflect on how you feel. See if your relationship with them changes.

When a child has a support worker working with them on an individual basis, the relationship between them can be very intense. It is sometimes the children that most need help with relationships, either with children or adults, that have support workers and this can contribute to the need for extra help and guidance for the member of staff working in this role in school. They play a valuable part in ensuring that children are able to reach their full potential, but the role is not without its difficulties. For example, a child may find it hard to settle and engage when the support worker is not there or may be jealous or find it hard to share them with other children in the class. It is crucial that their role is clearly explained to both the child and worker to ensure that these situations are easier to deal with.

Building relationships

It is worthwhile exploring what opportunities exist in school to build relationships between staff and children and how these can be increased. For some children, the experience of spending individual time with a member of school staff may seem terrifying. These children may have experienced adult relationships as being unpredictable and inconsistent and have developed this avoidance as a coping strategy and a way of feeling safe. They need to be able to experiment being in close proximity to an adult while still feeling safe and in control. A useful way to provide this can be to offer them the opportunity to choose a friend to do a job for you with them. This gives them permission to be as close or distant from you as they need to be. Gradually over time, as they develop a relationship with you, they may become more relaxed and be able to initiate contact for themselves. It is essential that they are encouraged to build the relationship themselves and that it is not rushed, as this may result in them feeling anxious and overwhelmed. All school staff have a responsibility to consider children who have difficulty building relationships and identify who could be made available and what could be done to help them when they feel scared or anxious in order to help them feel safe and secure. If this is overlooked and not prioritised, it can seriously affect children's ability to fully engage with their learning. Positive relational experiences are a basic human need and should not be used as a punishment or a reward in our schools. A sense of security with an adult in school is essential to a child's social and emotional development and emotional well-being.

Staff strategy – have I encouraged the children I work with to feel good about themselves today?

- Have I praised them?
- Have I acknowledged positive behaviour?
- Have I identified helpful hands?
- Have I recognised both effort and achievement in children's work?

Staff leaving

When a member of school staff leaves the school either during or at the end of the school year, this can have a big impact on some children. It is important for schools to consider how this is communicated to the children and when they are told. Some children develop close relationships with school staff and are devastated when they leave. It can be a huge loss for them and needs to be managed with thought and sensitivity. Children need to be given plenty of notice, rather than being told on the day the person is leaving. The ending needs to be marked in some way and the children offered the opportunity to make cards or draw pictures if they wish to. They need clear and honest explanations and the chance to ask questions in order to understand what is happening. When children have experienced adults coming in and out of their lives or just disappearing overnight due to relationship breakdown, it is essential that schools provide them with a supportive and reassuring experience of an ending with an adult.

How do children experience school staff?

As I discussed earlier in this chapter, each child brings their own template of relationships to school with them based on their experiences outside school. The relationships with staff at school can provide an alternative template for some children. For children who have developed vigilance as a way of feeling safe, they may notice non-verbal as well as verbal responses to situations. For example, does a member of staff frequently stand with their arms folded, frown regularly or look cross? What may this communicate to a child? Young children are very tuned in to non-verbal communication, and facial expressions and tone of voice are important emotional cues that are learned as a baby. In order for school staff to develop positive relationships, they need to be aware of the significance of every interaction with children.

Reflect: How approachable are you?

- Do you smile at children when you see them?
- Do you show children you can be trusted?
- Do you show interest in the children?
- Do you encourage children to talk to you if they want to?
- Do you listen when children talk to you?
- Do you support children with their feelings?

The acknowledgement of your role in school can also help to support this process; for example, offering help to a child by saying, 'Sometimes adults can help you with things', or, 'My job is to keep you safe,' to a child who is being bullied. These responses are particularly important for children who have learned self-sufficiency as a coping mechanism in order to feel safe. If staff listen to children's thoughts, ideas and opinions they feel heard, listened to and valued and may be more inclined to repeat this behaviour. If a child lives with fear and anxiety, they do not have inner peace and calm and may experience the world as unpredictable and dangerous. School staff may unconsciously reinforce this belief by responding in unpredictable and reactive ways to children. When school staff respond to children's anxieties and fears with compassion and understanding, rather than dismissing them as silly or inconsequential, they are validating the child's experience and enabling them to feel safe and supported at school. For example, 'I can see you look worried: maybe you think you won't get a turn on the bike, but Jamie will go round the track two more times and then it will be your go.' This response acknowledges and names the child's anxiety and explains what will happen next, thereby helping to ease it.

It is essential that staff take responsibility for and acknowledge their own mistakes and apologise when they get things wrong. We cannot expect children to do this if we are not able to do this as adults. The experience of making mistakes and getting things wrong without being shamed, humiliated or experiencing disapproval is a key factor in children being able to persevere and try again with tasks. This can be achieved by providing strong and consistent relational experiences with adults in school who can support and nurture them, along with adults modelling how they deal with making their own mistakes.

When children interrupt staff frequently and find it hard to wait to be listened to, this may be an indication that they do not get heard at home. It is important to be aware of how children who interrupt are responded to in school – are they criticised or humiliated, thereby evoking feelings of shame for the child, or responded to in an understanding way? It is very difficult for children (and some adults) to not say what comes into their head immediately. It is helpful and supportive to a child's confidence and self-esteem if they can be praised for being patient rather than penalised for being impatient.

During the group work programme, I acknowledge a child interrupting by saying, 'It's hard to wait when you have something you want to say, but we will just listen to Aiden and then it will be your turn', or I focus on their ability to be patient by saying, 'Well done for waiting for your turn; that can be a hard thing to do.' These responses support the child in trying to change their behaviour, rather than a punitive response that may make them feel uncomfortable.

When children feel that their opinion matters it enables them to formulate their own ideas, to make decisions and to value what they think. When children are encouraged to try new things and share their ideas and these are responded to in a positive way by school staff, it provides a message that they are important. This is essential for the development of confidence and self-esteem and to cultivate a strong sense of self-worth.

What are staff modelling by their relationships with each other?

Throughout the school day staff are interacting with each other and working together or alongside each other. School staff are provided with endless opportunities to model positive ways of interacting and demonstrate harmonious working relationships. It is useful to consider the relationships between staff and the messages they provide to the children; for example, does a child think, 'Miss Jones must hate Mrs Sullivan; she's always moaning about her'. This response is not only unprofessional and inappropriate for a child to witness, it also communicates about how to manage conflict, i.e. just moan rather than talk to the person and try and work out what the problem is. Adults working with children have a responsibility to demonstrate appropriate ways of expressing and dealing with their own feelings, for example, sharing excitement about a school trip.

What message does the following behaviour communicate to children?

- Staff being negative about each other.
- Staff snapping at each other.
- Staff challenging each other in an aggressive manner.
- Staff asking each other for help.
- Staff providing help to each other.

- Staff supporting and encouraging each other.
- Staff being relaxed with each other.
- Staff respecting each other.
- Staff valuing each other's opinions.
- Staff communicating easily and clearly to each other.

Reflect: Do staff walk their talk?

- Do school staff behave as they expect the children to?

When children are trying to navigate their way around their life at home with unpredictable and inconsistent parenting, they do not have a map to help them make sense of it. At school they are provided with a clear map in terms of rules and boundaries, but may need additional help understanding and following it. The school staff's increased awareness of this need for some children enables them to provide opportunities to support them with this throughout the school day. If children feel happy, safe, settled, valued and secure in school, then with the support of school staff they are able to be focused and ready to learn. They have the capacity to reach their full potential. How many children in your school feel like this every day and what can you do to improve it?

6 You can make a difference

The vital role that school staff play in contributing to children's emotional well-being cannot be underestimated and can be utilised more to ensure it is maximised to its full capacity. Every adult who works in a school has a responsibility to support children's emotional health and well-being and contribute to ensuring they feel good about themselves on a daily basis. The quality of the relationship between adults and children is crucial and every interaction can have a positive and meaningful outcome. As I discussed in Chapter 5, everything you say and do can affect children in either a positive or negative way: it can either enhance or erode their self-esteem and sense of self. We need to consider carefully what we say and how we say it, as this can have a big impact on a child. Our facial expression, body language and tone of voice all have meaning and will be interpreted by the child who is on the receiving end. This is of vital importance for children who are tuned in to adults' every move. They can be vigilant at trying to translate every movement and gesture, as well as the actual words that are spoken. When children have had negative experiences of how adults perceive them, they are especially competent at looking for evidence to validate this negative view of themselves. Mannerisms such as an adult waving their arms around, even in excitement, can cause anxiety and increase stress levels for children who live with unpredictability. The use of a gentle tone can go a long way in establishing a safe relationship for a child who is anxious and scared.

Reflect: Think about the changes you can make

- What can I do to make a difference to a child in school today?
- Will this make a small difference to me but a big difference to a child?
- How committed am I to making a difference to a child's life?

Try alternative ways to respond to children's behaviour

Throughout this book I have been encouraging school staff to try different strategies to deal with children's behaviour. It can be easy in life to keep doing things the way we've always done them and harder to be brave enough to experiment with another way. However, as has been discussed in the previous chapters, the significant relationships between school staff and children that can occur in school settings enable both children and staff to experiment with this concept. The more that school staff can get to know and understand the children in their care, the more they will be able to develop appropriate responses to behaviour to meet the child's needs.

Case study

Hannah, aged 4, found it very hard to sit on a chair at school. She would lean from side to side, sit up on her knees and rock on it, occasionally falling off.

Teacher response

Her class teacher understood that this was something that Hannah found difficult and needed help with and acknowledged this to her by saying, 'I can see it's really hard for you to sit still on your chair; I'm wondering if we should spend some time together to see if I can help to make it easier for you.' The teacher spent time showing Hannah where to put her feet so they could be settled comfortably on the floor and explored with her how this felt.

Result

Hannah responded to this help from her teacher by becoming more aware of how she was sitting and with gentle reminders such as, 'I'm wondering if you need a bit more help with your chair?' was able to manage sitting more easily.

While this teacher response may not have had the same effect with other children, if school staff are able to think for a minute before responding to behaviour, they may be able to adapt their responses to meet the child's individual needs. This may result in the child feeling more understood and have a positive outcome for both staff and child.

Focus on behavioural expectations

Sometimes addressing the class as a whole or wondering aloud can be a useful way of supporting individual children to try and change their behaviour and can be less punitive than targeting individual children. For example, when the noise in the class is increasing it can be helpful to use a bell or a tambourine as a gentle way of getting everyone's attention and acknowledge this by saying, 'It's quite noisy and I'm just wondering if we can try and use our quiet voices.' This suggestion clearly communicates a behavioural expectation for the whole class and provides gentle ways of helping children to achieve this. The behavioural change can then be acknowledged and praised with, 'That's much better. Well done for making the change I asked for.' When all children are clear about the behavioural expectations that school staff have of them, it may make it easier for them to work together and support one another in achieving this. The focus and validation of the behaviour that you would like to see, rather than the behaviour that you don't, provides a positive reinforcement to all children. This is particularly important for children who have the opposite experience of this outside school, as they are able to achieve a level of success and sense of accomplishment in school, increasing the desire for them to repeat this behaviour.

Staff strategy – to help engage the whole class on the carpet

'Who can I see that looks ready to listen? Who can I see that looks ready for learning?'

This strategy is a gentle way of reminding the class of a behavioural expectation you have of them giving you their attention when you ask for it.

Spend extra time with children

Investing just five minutes a day with a child can have a huge impact. I have encouraged school staff to do this at lunchtime, while they are clearing up or setting out the class, and it has provided children with a different experience of a staff relationship. The child can be involved in helping put out equipment or tidying the pencils and it enables an informal interaction to take place and the relationship to develop. The message it gives to children is positive, as it validates who they are. The outcome for the child is beneficial in terms of relationship experience and developing confidence and self-esteem. The sense of purpose and importance developed by offering children the opportunity to help with jobs enables them to feel better about themselves. However, a note of caution is necessary to ensure that children do not feel they are only of value or importance when they are helping other people, so this needs to be considered when identifying children who may benefit from this additional input.

Reflect: What do I do?

- How often do I show interest in the children?
- Do I remember things they tell me?
- Do I remember to ask them about things they have told me?

Be a significant adult

One of the joys of working in schools can be the opportunity to build relationships in an informal manner with children. These snapshot conversations that take place during the day and give us an insight into children's lives are so important for our relationship building. It can be very difficult to retain any of this information, let alone remember to ask about it again. However, if we are able to do this it can have a huge impact. As adults we know how it feels if someone remembers to ask us about something we have shared with them – we feel listened to, understood and validated for being important and worth thinking about and remembering. Imagine how powerful this would feel to a child, especially a child who is not used to this happening, and imagine how good it may make them feel. For a child who is not used to adults outside school showing them much interest, it can make them feel special and interesting if an adult in school asks them whether the dog is better now or how their new baby brother is doing.

Reflect: Draw the path of your life

- On a large sheet of paper, draw the path of your life from the age of 5 up to now.
- Include significant situations, events and people.
- Reflect on where and how the people influenced you.
- What did they say and do?
- How did they make you feel?
- Can you do that for a child at school now?

Provide positive messages to children

I am sure we can all remember significant people that have had an influence on our lives. They may have impacted on the way we think and view things or the choices we now make in our lives. When I was 10, I remember my class teacher taking me to the staff room with her when she had her preparation time, as I was too disruptive to be left in the class without her. She used to draw lines in pencil to divide the lines in my book and I had to try and write underneath the bottom line to help me practise my handwriting, which was very untidy. I remember feeling very important, pleased that she wanted to help me, and determined to improve my handwriting. My writing changed significantly for the better that year because of the time and commitment my teacher gave me and the messages she provided about wanting to help me.

Staff strategy – choose a child

Choose a child you feel would benefit from some extra adult input in their lives. Choose one thing you could do each day for a week to provide a positive message to them. You can use ideas from the list below or think of your own alternatives:

- Ask them if they would like to help you do a job with their friend.
- Acknowledge something positive about them.
- Remember something about them and share it with them.
- Ask something about them.

Don't underestimate the crucial role you can play in changing a child's experience of life and relationships. It may not be noticeable immediately or measurable straight away, but you never know what seeds you have planted or when they will grow. All school staff have a responsibility to invest time, thought, energy and commitment into exploring how they can contribute to and enhance children's emotional well-being on a daily basis. Every member of school staff has a role to play in helping children reach their full potential. You have to believe you can make a difference and start making it today.

Think of Jim

From 0–10 years Jim hears what a bad person he is at home every day. His behaviour at school is challenging and disruptive. The school staff find it hard to manage his behaviour and unconsciously reinforce the messages he has received at home, that he is a bad person.

From 10–20 years Jim struggles with friendships and relationships and is often in trouble with the police.

From 20–30 years Jim criticises and struggles to manage his own children's behaviour and to have a good relationship with them.

From 30–40 years Jim's kids don't want to see him and he is drinking heavily to drown out the internal voice that keeps telling him he's a bad person.

- Imagine if at age 4 Jim had been a pupil at your school.
- Imagine if he had been flooded with messages that told him he was a good person.
- Imagine if he had experienced the school staff as showing him he was a worthwhile person who had good qualities to share with the world.
- Imagine if he had taken that confidence and self-esteem and positive sense of himself with him when he left the school.
- Imagine what his life could have been like at age 20, 30 or 40.
- Imagine if he had been lucky enough to come to your school.

Making schools happier places

Reflect: Stop for a minute

Ask yourself the following questions:

- Why did I want to work in a school?
- What did I want to achieve?
- Have I achieved this?
- What can I do tomorrow to make the school a happier place for the children?

In order to make a school a happier place for the children, parents and staff who use it, each member of school staff could contribute one small thing every day. This can contribute to changing the atmosphere and ethos of the school and is achievable by everyone showing a commitment. The quality of the relationships between children, parents and staff can change by smiling as you walk around the school. I work in several different schools during the week and certainly do not know the names of all the children and parents, but I smile at them as I walk around the school. I acknowledge children if they hold open a door for me (which they do frequently) by saying, 'Thanks for holding the door open for me; that's very kind of you', or, 'That's thoughtful of you.' This enables the child to know that I not only appreciate them holding the door, but I also experience them as being kind or thoughtful. How often do we see children showing us kind, caring, thoughtful behaviour in school but choose not to acknowledge it or are too busy to do so? Let's commit to changing this and providing children with positive feelings about who they are and what they do as often as we can during each school day. If we believe in children, we enable them to believe in themselves.

Every child has the right to be happy, settled and achieving their full potential in school. Is this true for every child in your school? If not, is there anything you can do to make a difference?

Part Two: Practice

Using group work to promote emotional health and well-being and manage children's behaviour

7 The benefits of group work

The second section of this book explores the group work programmes that involve a focused approach to help children to deal with many of the issues discussed in the first section of the book. The group work sessions provide a safe and structured environment that enables children to practise and develop new skills. The friendship group supports children who require additional support in developing and sustaining friendships, managing relationships, and dealing with conflict. The self-esteem group supports children who require additional support to develop confidence and self-esteem. Children can develop both sets of skills from participating in either programme, both of which also contribute to development and resilience. The group work programme in this book is carefully structured and the activities are clear, simple and easy to follow, because the focus is on the relationships within the group and enabling children to make changes in their behaviour.

The group facilitator can ensure that certain concepts are introduced each week if they will support the development of new skills for the children – for example, introducing the idea of waiting, if the children are finding this difficult to do. The exploratory manner used by the facilitator to introduce this idea enables a discussion to take place about the meaning of the word and how the group can use it. This child-focused approach may result in a clearer understanding and more willing implementation from the children.

Opportunity to change behaviour

The experience of being part of a small group in a safe and supportive environment provides children with the opportunity to experiment with alternative ways of behaving, if they wish to. The group facilitator encourages this process by offering praise and encouragement, along with acknowledging how difficult it can be to make changes.

Case study

Emily, aged 4, was very quiet in the group – she found it difficult to participate and spoke in a very soft voice, so it was hard to hear and understand her. The other child sometimes spoke for her and appeared to find it hard to wait for her to get her words out.

Possible reasons for Emily's behaviour:

- There was a history of drug and alcohol abuse in her family.
- She had recently been taken into foster care and had become even more quiet and withdrawn.

The teaching assistant who was facilitating the group commented on Emily's struggle and acknowledged this by reflecting, 'Sometimes it can be really hard to speak, but remember in here you can share your ideas if you want to, and if you don't want to, that's okay. We can all help you with this.' This reflection acknowledged the difficulty she was having and encouraged her to try and practise within the group. This enabled Emily to use the experience of being in the group as an opportunity to practise changing behaviour that she found difficult. On the last week the activity involved making an 'I am proud of me' badge, with discussions about what 'proud' meant and when we might feel like this. When Emily was given her folder to take, she said, 'I am proud of my folder because there's a lot' (meaning there were lots of things in her folder). This demonstrated her understanding of the concept of being proud and an increase in her confidence and self-esteem.

The support and acceptance provided by the other child in the group and the facilitator enabled Emily to experiment with a new behaviour in a safe environment. The facilitator was able to see and acknowledge her progress each week and comment, 'You are doing so well at telling us your ideas, Emily. I know that's a really hard thing to do.' This encouraged Emily to persevere and make changes to her behaviour.

The experience of being in the small group enabled her to practise and become competent at adjusting to an expectation of school and society in general, i.e. speaking to others. The predictable format of the sessions provided her with a sense of stability that enabled her to feel safe to experiment with making changes within the group. The facilitator's encouragement and understanding of Emily's behaviour helped to connect rather than separate them as they worked alongside each other to facilitate this change. This increased self-confidence within the group setting increased as the sessions progressed and became noticeable to her class teacher and foster carer outside the group.

The following examples are taken from children in schools who have experienced the group work programme:

Table 7.1 Impact of group work programme

Behaviour before the group	Behaviour after the group
Needing frequent adult attention	More confident and less demanding of adult attention
Unwilling to try and do things themselves	Happy to try and do things for themselves
Not contributing their ideas to class discussions	Happy to share their thoughts and ideas
Shouting out all the time	Able to wait their turn with gentle reminders
Being quiet and reserved	Speaking out and being more confident
Frequently saying they feel unwell	No longer saying they feel unwell unless they are
Interrupting frequently	Able to wait their turn
Easily distracted and poor concentration	Improved concentration and attention span
Restless and fidgety	More settled and focused
Regular tantrums and angry outbursts	Calmer and happier in themselves

Belonging and ownership

The experience of being in a group with the same people enables the children to feel a sense of ownership and belonging that is particularly important for children who may not have this experience at home. Some children may encounter feelings of loneliness, isolation and rejection both at home and school, and the chance to be part of something on a weekly basis may help with this. This sense of belonging and feeling that they have something of value to contribute may enable them to develop positive feelings about themselves, resulting in increased confidence and self-esteem.

Children want and need:

- to be accepted;
- to be valued;
- to feel they have something to offer;
- to feel good about themselves.

Consistency

The group is held at the same time on the same day and in the same place each week, for example, Monday 10–10.20am in the Resource room. This consistency and predictability can reduce anxiety levels for the children and help them to feel safer in school. The sessions are clearly structured with a beginning, middle and end activity each week. The focus on time and acknowledging to the children when they have a few minutes left, if they are involved in making something, provides a sense of reliability as they know what will happen, rather than finishing abruptly, which can increase anxiety. The sessions start and end in the same way each week with the main activity changing, enabling the children to adjust to being back in the group by providing them with something familiar. This structure and regularity is crucial to the group work programme and the sense of belonging that is developed by the children. It provides an opportunity to be able to respond to organisation and predictable routines, which some of the children may not have much experience of. This also helps them to feel secure and more settled in school, often resulting in them being able to manage the time outside the group more effectively.

The activities and sessions are planned and organised in a way that enables the children to practise new skills, such as sharing, taking turns and working together. They discuss topics such as feeling proud, waiting for their turn, and having friends, validating and affirming the feelings that may be evoked by these. Children can experience the peer reactions to the situations that occur in the group as a way of normalising their behaviour, with reflections and commentary from the facilitator. 'Joe looked a bit cross that Sunita went first, but remember that you will both have a turn to go first in this group.' The development of self-control is a process that lasts a lifetime, and the more opportunities that children have to develop self-awareness with the support of a nurturing adult, the increased likelihood of them developing the skills for themselves. All these skills are crucial factors in the development of resilience.

Choices and consequences

The sessions provide children with the opportunity to understand about choices and consequences and the impact of these on the others in the group, as well as themselves. They are encouraged to think about and share how they feel about making and giving things to each other, and the facilitator is encouraged to address negative comments or criticisms in an open and honest way.

For example, when carrying out the activity of decorating a butterfly for the other person (Week 5, Friendship programme), Taylor, aged 4, said 'Ella, I don't like blue I want it to be green'. The facilitator reflected by saying, 'It can feel really difficult when someone is making something for us and we are not happy with it or feel we would have liked it to be done differently, but in here we are practising new things.' The development of understanding and compassion for others is a crucial part of children learning self-acceptance and self-compassion. The opportunity to experience this within an emotionally safe and nurturing small group environment increases their understanding and the likelihood of them implementing it outside the group setting.

Developing new skills

The activities enable the children to gain a sense of achievement and the focus is on the effort made and the process, rather than the end product. They are designed to help the children experience success and gain mastery through challenge and perseverance. This is supported by focused help from the group facilitator, if needed. This development of new skills may be transferred outside the group where other tasks may be greeted with effort and determination, rather than helplessness and resignation to failure. The tasks are planned to promote the skills we want the children to develop. For example, making a model together (Week 4, Friendship programme) that involves the children each taking turns to choose a brick and deciding where they would like to put it on the model. This activity brings a variety of reactions about control from the children and provides an ideal opportunity to enable them to understand this, have their feelings acknowledged and practising new skills such as compromise, sharing and negotiating. The activities provide an opportunity for the facilitator to discuss these concepts with them, check their understanding and provide feedback to their class teacher about any challenges or successes that may occur with the children during this process.

Validating feelings

An important role of the facilitator is to validate feelings and through the activities acknowledge that all feelings are acceptable. For example, Week 3 of the Friendship programme and Week 2 of the Self-esteem programme both involve activities that encourage the children to explore and talk about different feelings. This enables the children to develop more understanding of their own feelings, and the safe environment created by the facilitator encourages the children to discuss this in a more relaxed way, gradually sharing their own if they choose to as they become more confident. However, while the sessions encourage the children to share their own thoughts and feelings, they are also given permission not to do this if they feel uncomfortable. This is crucial in ensuring that children feel safe and comfortable within the sessions and are able to choose when and how they contribute.

Case study

Kaiden, aged 4, was in a friendship group and had witnessed domestic violence and had recently moved house and school. At first he would just point to the expression face he had chosen at the end of each session without speaking, but with support and encouragement from the facilitator he began to name the feeling and became more vocal. In Week 3, when doing an activity on feelings and talking about feeling scared, he said, 'People can be scary, people can shout.'

The caring and nurturing response from the group facilitator enabled Kaiden to feel safe and to gradually be able to start voicing his experience. Initially in class he was very quiet but vigilant to what was happening around him; his experience of being in the group enabled him to slowly develop a friendship with another child and begin to relax and develop confidence. It can sometimes be easy for children such as Kaiden to go unnoticed in class as they may not present challenging behaviour or disrupt the class. However, these children need help just as much as the children who are showing confrontational behaviour, often more so as they may be more easily overlooked.

As mentioned before, both programmes also involve an activity where each child makes something for the other child in the group. This provides an ideal opportunity to explore how it feels to make something for someone else and what feelings it may activate. They are encouraged to thank each other for making something and then explore how it feels when someone thanks you for something you have done for them. This enables the development of new skills, both personally and socially, as well as providing the opportunity to experience sharing feelings in a positive and welcoming environment.

At the end of each session they are asked to look at four pictures showing facial expressions of sad, happy, cross and worried and encouraged to choose one and identify and share how they feel, if they want to.

Table 7.2 Examples of experiences shared by children at the end of the session

Facial expression shows	Reason given by child
Happy	I like it in here
Sad	I hurt my finger
Cross	Mummy wouldn't buy me a toy
Worried	It was dark

This opportunity to explore, name and share their feelings in a safe and supportive environment enables them to practise doing this and helps them to become more emotionally articulate outside the sessions.

Building relationships

The experience of delivering group work provides the facilitator with the opportunity to focus on and get to know the children in a more relaxed way, along with enabling them to build a connection and get to know them better. The building of strong relationships with children gives powerful messages to them that school staff will support them and help them with their behaviour if they need it.

The group work opportunity also provides a chance for children who struggle with and/or actively avoid adult relationships to have a more intimate experience of this. This can feel safer and less intense as another child is present and the relationship can be developed gradually in a more diluted way. It enables staff to relate to the children in a more relaxed way, to enjoy their personality and get to know and acknowledge their qualities, as well as offering a high level of support and attention.

Staff development

The school staff who deliver the groups are able to gain awareness of how they relate to the children and learn new skills to improve their relationships. They also increase their perception of how they communicate with children, along with gaining a deeper understanding of children's emotional and social development. For example, Kathy was a very skilled teaching assistant who was good at building relationships with the children. However, she admitted that she sometimes struggled with developing and maintaining boundaries with the children, especially around finishing time if they were enjoying doing something. Her activities in class often ran over and she acknowledged that her time management was poor.

The experience of delivering the group work enabled her to practise new ways of working and to practise working to the times allocated for the activities. The 5-minute warning she gave to the children before they finished the main activity allowed her to see that the children were happy with this as long as they knew what was happening and why. It enabled her to gain a better understanding of some of the emotional reactions and behaviour she had experienced from children in the past when she had expected them to just stop what they were doing. She transferred this time warning to the activities she carried out in class and was pleased to experience the results from the children being the same. It also helped her to improve an aspect of her work.

Delivering the group work programme provides the facilitator with an ideal opportunity to develop new skills that can be transferred to their role outside the group. The heightened awareness of children's emotional needs and the use of reflective language can be integrated into the facilitator's existing role in school in a way that promotes their confidence and enhances their contribution to the rest of the staff team.

Positive messages

The use of reflective language throughout the group work sessions provides the children with a very positive message about themselves as it communicates, 'I can see you, I am trying to understand you, whatever you are thinking or feeling is okay, you are worth thinking about and I am interested in getting to know you.' All these responses reinforce that the child is important as an individual in their own right and provides a clear sense of acceptance of who they are as a person. The programme promotes an awareness of the children's own emotions along with sensitivity to the emotions of other people, resulting in an increased ability to put those feelings into words. The experience of the group work programmes and the facilitator's reflections given to the children are positive and powerful and, for some children, may provide new opportunities for them to be experienced in this way. The facilitator's use of reflective language enables the children to feel seen, heard, valued and understood – all essential ingredients to build their confidence and self-esteem.

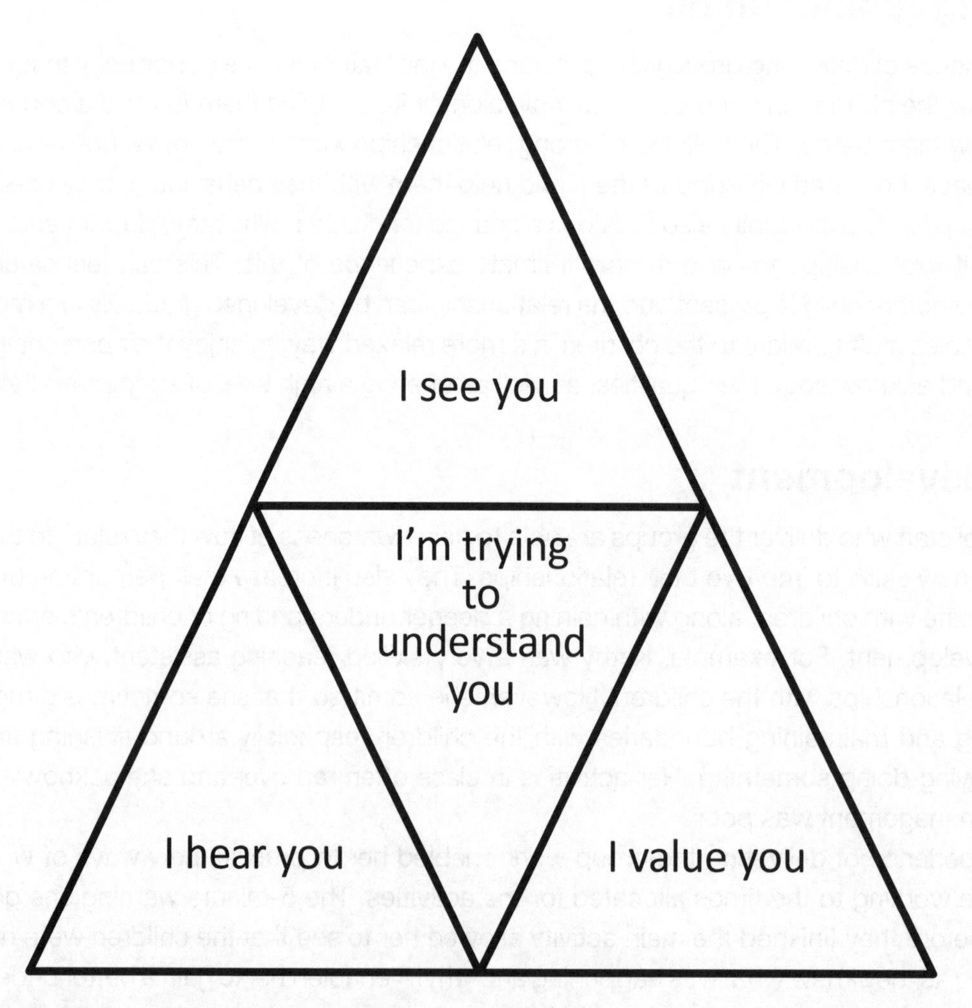

Figure 7.1 Positive messages to children

Communication skills

The group work provides an opportunity to develop children's social and communication skills and enables some children to find their voice for the first time, while others can practise being less domineering towards other people.

Case study

Ellie, aged 5, was referred to the self-esteem group by her class teacher who found her difficult because she was constantly talking, calling out and telling the other children what to do. This was impacting on her learning and friendships, as the other children in the class were wary of her and avoided her if they could. Ellie showed this behaviour in the group work sessions, and in week 3, when exploring the feely bag, as she found it very hard to let the other child have a turn and not to intervene.

However, with reflections such as, 'I can see it's difficult to wait while Kyra has a turn, but I wonder what it would be like to let her finish', or, 'Well done for waiting; I know that's a hard thing to do', she was gradually able to wait for longer. As she knew she would have her turn eventually, this lessened her anxiety and enabled her to practise patience and self-regulation. I spoke to her class teacher and encouraged her to try this reflection with her in class and she was pleased with the results and found she was calling out far less than she had been before participating in the programme.

New opportunities

There are children in our schools who have learned to hide themselves and their needs and instead have developed a way of being that puts everyone else's needs before their own. These children are often invisible in schools as their behaviour may not outwardly present as a concern, especially if there are a number of children who show their feelings in a more challenging way. The group work programmes provide an ideal opportunity for these otherwise invisible children to become more visible within the sessions and to start understanding and expressing their needs and wishes. There have been several examples of these children actively showing more confidence and having more of a presence in school.

Case study

Leah, aged 3, was very quiet and shy in class and rarely spoke to adults or children. For the first two sessions in the self-esteem group she was very cautious and was constantly watching the other child start before doing something herself. Each week she struggled by herself to put her session chart on her folder, shaking her head at any offers of help. As the facilitator began acknowledging the potential feelings and reflecting on her behaviour, Leah gradually began participating more. The facilitator reflected on her struggles to do things on her own and said, 'I wonder what it would be like for you to let me help you with your folder.' Leah responded by handing her the folder, and although she looked unsure, allowed the facilitator to help her. By the last session she was confidently helping herself to the pens and colouring in her session chart as soon as she came into the room. She also smiled when she explored the contents of her folder.

Her class teacher noticed that she began making more eye contact and began approaching adults if she needed help – all indicators of an increase in her confidence and self-esteem, as well as the development of trust in the school staff.

The early messages some children receive about not being seen or heard may result in them finding it difficult to speak out in any situation and being quiet and withdrawn in an attempt not to draw attention to themselves. For these children, the group work programmes provide an ideal opportunity for them to practise finding their voice and sharing their thoughts and feelings within a smaller group, if they wish to. As these children develop more confidence in speaking in front of another child, these skills may then become transferable to the larger group within the classroom. The permissive and accepting environment created by the facilitator within the group sessions can enable children to feel noticed in a less threatening and exposing way than in a whole class situation. The reflective language used by the facilitator can enable the child to feel more confident in speaking out.

The group work experience may also benefit children who find it hard to make decisions for themselves. When adults are always in control and making choices for children, it is not surprising that children may present as helpless and unable to do this. The opportunities created by the group work experience enable children to make choices and decisions in the activities that are included, along with encouraging each child to have a voice and share their thoughts and ideas. For example, several activities encourage the children to decorate or make things using a range of materials, which they are encouraged to choose from. If a child finds this hard they are provided with additional reassurance and acknowledgement of their feelings by the group facilitator. For example, 'I can see you looking at all the things you can use; maybe you are unsure which to have. Remember, it's your folder and you can decorate it however you like.'

The group work experience introduces many new ideas and concepts to the children. Along with the development of social and emotional skills, it can also expand the children's vocabulary by introducing new words in the context of the sessions. For example, exploring what each of the feelings means and talking about being proud and how that may feel. This provides a useful opportunity to talk about how we may experience feelings in our body; for example, when we feel proud we may feel it in our tummy. This is particularly beneficial for younger children who experience their feelings as a bodily sensation and may feel frightened or overwhelmed by it.

Affirmative responses

Throughout the facilitator's guidelines I suggest reflecting, 'You may need some help from an adult with this, and I can help you if you would like me to.' This reflection provides the message that sometimes children need help from an adult and it is acceptable to ask for it. This is particularly important for children who have learned self-sufficiency at a young age and will struggle on their own as they have learned 'it's not okay to ask for help' or, 'even if you do, no one helps you'. It enables the child to have the choice and decide whether they need help, rather than the adult controlling the situation and deciding for them. I encourage the facilitator to say, 'help from an adult' as a generic term, rather than 'help from me', as this reinforces that other adults outside the group may also be able to help if they need it, and it gives the message that it's acceptable to ask them.

Positive changes in children

The benefits to the children of being in the group work sessions can become apparent to the facilitators as the sessions progress. They may see changes such as increased confidence, more willingness to speak out, being able to be patient while others speak. The class teachers have commented on improved concentration, improved peer relationships, more ability to recognise, express and manage their feelings, and more empathy towards others. Some children have identified and shared the benefits themselves such as, 'I like being in this group'. Some parents have also noticed the differences in their children since being in the group work sessions and have said, 'He's much more settled in school now', and, 'She's much calmer and can tell me if she's upset now'. These are examples of the visible impact – there may be many more that are less visible and that may only be noticed in specific situations, for example, being more able to cope with losing.

The overall experience of being part of the group cannot only be beneficial for school staff and individual children, but it can also highlight areas of concern and need for children that may otherwise be unnoticed. This provides the school with the opportunity to respond in a way that ensures they are meeting each child's emotional and social needs and promoting a whole school approach to children's mental health and well-being.

8 The role of the group facilitator

The group facilitator can be a learning mentor, teaching assistant, support worker, family worker or other role within the school who has a thorough understanding of children's social and emotional development and is confident working with small groups. They need to be interested in emotional well-being and developing new skills to manage children's behaviour, have a capacity for some self-reflection and a willingness to try using the reflective language skills described.

The groups are most effective when they are implemented following the clear time guidelines set out in the group work packs, as this enables the sessions to be structured and organised. The format is deliberately prescriptive and enables the facilitator to be exploratory with the children. There is a resource list for each six-week programme, and these must be ready at the start of each session before the children come in. It is useful to allocate 40 minutes to the facilitator for each group to allow for time to set out resources and clear away, reflect on the session and write brief session notes at the end of the group. They will also need some time to be allocated at the end of each six-week group to write a brief report on each child. This is discussed in more detail later in the chapter.

Completing questionnaires for the group

In order to maximise the benefits of the group work experience for the children, it is useful to complete a questionnaire for both children at the start and end of the intervention (see Resources section). This enables any changes that children have made to be monitored, along with identifying children who may benefit from additional support. The questionnaires are in the Resources section and can be photocopied for each child. They can be completed by the child's teacher or by a teaching assistant who knows the child well. It is important that the start and end questionnaires are completed by the same person, wherever possible. There is more information on how to complete the questionnaires in the group work questionnaires guidelines sheet in the Resources section.

Developing new relationships

The group work sessions provide the facilitator with an ideal opportunity to develop their relationship with the identified children and practise a new way of managing their behaviour by acknowledging and reflecting their feelings. For example, Dontay, aged four, was very unsure about participating in some of the activities during the group work sessions and needed lots of encouragement from the facilitator. During an activity using a feely bag, the facilitator was able to focus on his anxieties and acknowledge them by reflecting, 'I can see you look a bit unsure; maybe you are worried about not guessing what it is, but remember we can ask Oliver to help you and see if he knows. It can be hard to remember things sometimes, and in here we can help each other.' This response helped to reassure him and validated his feelings.

At the start of each session after setting out the folders and resources, the children are collected from their class and brought to the room. This is an important part of the process and gives a message of caring and nurture to the children. The children can be excited, scared and anxious at the start of the sessions, particularly the first one when they are unsure what will be happening. It can be useful to acknowledge this to them; for example, 'It may feel a bit strange coming out of class with me, but I will explain what we will be doing when we get to the room.' This can help to reduce any feelings of anxiety and fear. The use of reflections provides all the following positive messages to the children and can be a useful way to identify the impact of its use.

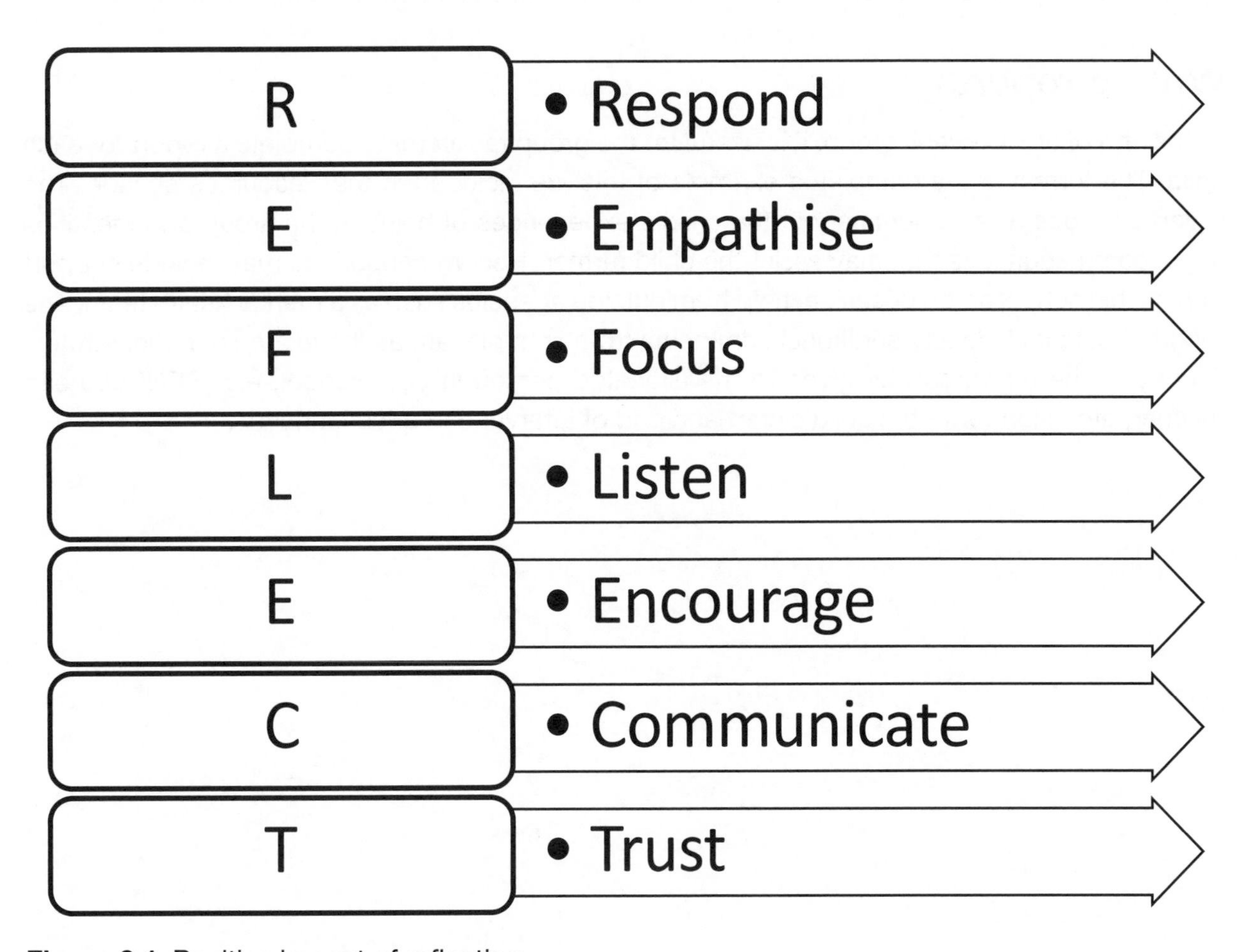

Figure 8.1 Positive impact of reflecting

Sharing information with other people

There may be opportunities to share relevant information with children's parents or carers, if this is appropriate. For example, if a child is trying hard to change their behaviour or has made a positive contribution to the group, it may be useful to share this with their parent. This information can be shared in order to highlight the effort the child is making and to enable the parent or carer to support this behaviour at home. It can also be useful to share relevant information with the children's class teacher on a weekly basis so they can follow the child's process. For example, sharing that a quiet child has spoken for the first time and how this occurred. If children appear to be responding to particular reflections, it is useful to share these with the class teacher who may also choose to use a similar response to help a child. Other school staff, including lunchtime organisers, teaching assistants and the head teacher may also benefit from receiving feedback on the changes a child is working on within the group, so they are able to support this and acknowledge it to the child, if appropriate.

Identifying children who may benefit from further support

The group work programme may identify children who need further intervention or specific, focused help with particular areas. The facilitator will need to share this information with a more senior member of staff within the school, such as the special educational needs co-ordinator (SENCO), in order to build on the work of the group where necessary. This can also be highlighted on the group work report under the section on recommendations. It is also essential that any concerns, for example, a child disclosing or child protection concerns, are recorded and passed on to the relevant member of staff, in line with the school's child protection procedure.

Writing reports

At the end of the six-week group, it is useful for the group facilitator to complete a report for each child. The format and a completed example of this are included in the Resources section. The report provides a short summary of the child's experiences of being in the group and identifies any recommendations that may assist the child further. Recommendations may include support from within school or, on occasion, help from outside agencies such as a mental health team. The report should include any additional comments from school staff, as the example demonstrates. A copy of the report can be given to the allocated person in your school, e.g. SENCO, head teacher, etc., along with the child's start and end of intervention questionnaires.

9 Starting and ending group work

The groups work well with two children of either the same gender or a girl and boy and are most effective if they are from the same class, as this maximises the opportunities for friendship outside the sessions. This provides a more intense and focused intervention, which can be useful for children who need extra support with sharing, waiting their turn, and other social and emotional skills. This enables them to achieve success within a more realistic environment, which can then encourage them to practise these skills outside the group on a weekly basis.

Group composition

It is also useful to consider the developmental levels of the children that are to be in the same group to ensure that they will be able to manage the tasks at a similar pace and level. The personalities of the children can be considered, too, so there are combinations of dominant and less dominant children who can both be provided with support to make changes to their behaviour. Children can participate in both of the group work programmes, but this would be most effective if there was a period of time in between to integrate the skills they have learned.

When considering the group composition it is essential to consider both children's individual needs to ensure the group's success and the children's emotional safety. It is aimed at children who are low-level disrupters and children who would benefit from additional, focused support, rather than children who have more complex needs and may require more specialised intervention. If a child presents with very challenging behaviour and has complex needs, then being in a group may be too intense and overwhelming, resulting in the child sabotaging the group as a way of managing their feelings. This may enable them to practise different ways of behaving and have this modelled for them in a nurturing environment.

Children who may benefit from the group work programme include:

- children who lack confidence or have low self-esteem;
- children who find it hard to make friends;
- children who are quiet and withdrawn;
- children who are pleasers and feel their own needs are not important;
- children who interrupt and find it hard to listen;
- children who find it hard to share and take turns;
- children who tell lies;
- children who find it hard to make mistakes;
- children who have regular conflict with other children;
- children who bully others or who are bullied themselves;
- children who are restless and find it hard to concentrate;
- children who are anxious, worried or fearful;
- children who lack resilience;
- children who have tantrums;
- children who are experiencing changes at home, such as a new baby, etc.

The group is an ideal opportunity to boost children who are not as happy or settled as they could be, or who are not achieving their full potential.

Format of the sessions

The sessions are held for 20 minutes once a week for six weeks. As mentioned in previous chapters, it is an essential part of the process that it is held at the same time, same day and in the same room each week, as this models consistency, predictability and provides structure to their week. The room must be available each week and have a mat or rug on the floor to identify the space you will be using. Ideally, this can be a small room where there may be minimal external distractions to enable the children to focus on the group. It is ESSENTIAL that the group is not disturbed by other people who need resources from the room or wish to use it, as this can be very disruptive and gives a message that the group is not important. A sign on the door at the start of the session (see Resources section) and a reminder at staff meetings can ensure there are no interruptions.

The room needs to convey a positive and welcoming message to the children as they enter it. The physical and emotional environment that is being provided by the group work is crucial to its success and impact. For some children, whose lives outside school may be chaotic and unpredictable, the calm, tidy and peaceful environment will enable them to feel safe and to settle more easily. It is also useful if there is limited equipment in the room to minimise distractions for the children, although this is not always possible. They may be more aware of their physical and emotional environment and therefore the group work setting can provide an opportunity to relax and enjoy their time in the group.

Starting something new can make some children feel very anxious and scared. It is important that this is acknowledged (see facilitator's guidelines for session 1, Chapter 11 and 12 for reflections to use). If a child looks anxious or uncertain, it may be due to hyper vigilance, and it is crucial that this is acknowledged. If the facilitator reflects on this and notices what the child is doing and says, 'I can see you looking at all the collage materials; maybe you're wondering what we are going to do in here today – I'll tell you when we are all sitting down', this provides a strong message of acknowledgement and validation to the child, along with reassuring them.

When the children have sat down in their spaces chosen by the facilitator, explain to them that this is a group that will meet every week in the same room for six weeks for 20 minutes and show them the start and end times on the clock. It can be useful to use a small paper arrow to indicate the start and end times to make this clearer to them. Explain the group will meet at the same time and on the same day each week, and that if you are absent then they will not lose that session; it will be carried out the following week when you are back in school, and explain that this will also happen if one of them is not in school. Explain that the group will start and end in the same way each week and there will be a different activity in the middle. Discuss that the group is a way of helping them to practise and develop new skills, such as sharing and taking turns, and that the activities will provide ways to help them with this. The facilitator's guidelines (see Chapter 11 and Chapter 12) provide detailed, step by step information for each session, and it is useful to read these in advance of the sessions to ensure they are understood and can be followed easily. They provide clear explanations for the beginning, middle and end of each session, along with suggested reflections that may be useful to use with the children.

The facilitator must ensure they follow the time guidelines set out in the group work pack, as this will enable the group to run smoothly. At the end of the session, acknowledge their hard work, tell them you will see them next week and walk them back to their class. The facilitator needs some time at the end of each session to complete the register and session detail sheet (see

Resources section). The session detail sheet will provide a brief overview of how the facilitator feels the session went and a few sentences on each child, such as 'The children both enjoyed making the model together and Jamaal was able to await his turn more easily. Kai said he felt happy today because he was seeing his dad after school.'

Both children will be given a folder of the same colour for them to keep the activities in. They will also have a session chart to colour that shows how many sessions they are having and provides a structured beginning to each week as they colour in the appropriate number chart (see Resources section).

They keep the session chart in their folder and these are set out for them on the floor when they come to each session and need to be in the same place each week to ensure consistency. The group facilitator keeps the folders and their contents in a safe place until the last session when the children can take them home if they want to. As this is explained to the group at the start of the first session, most children are okay with this. If a child finds this difficult, it may tell us something about their experience of trust and can be reflected to them; for example, 'It seems that you're really not sure about me looking after your folder – maybe it's hard for you to leave it with me, but that's one of our rules and I will keep it safe for you.'

This concept may be difficult for the children to grasp, but it is a useful one in terms of them developing trust with the facilitator and understanding about the continuity of the sessions. After the first one or two sessions they are usually happy to do this and may comment on the fact they will be taking it home on the last week.

Each session starts and ends in a similar way each week, with an activity in the middle. It is useful to show the children on the clock how long they will spend with you so they are aware of this and learn to manage the time. They will become familiar with the structure of the sessions very quickly, and the predictability provides them with a sense of security.

Although there are no specific rules for the group, it is useful to identify and reflect on specific behavioural issues as they occur. For example, 'I can see you really want to go first, Jane, but in here we are going to practise doing things that we find difficult. When Joe has had his turn, then it will be your go. I know it can feel hard, but let's see if you are able to wait.'

If a child seems uncomfortable or reluctant to participate, then it is important that they are gently guided to do this, with their possible feelings being acknowledged. For example, 'I can see you look unsure about talking in here, maybe it feels a bit uncomfortable and sometimes it can be difficult to share. Maybe it's too hard today and that's okay.' Once the sessions have progressed and the children are familiar with the format and feel relaxed, they are usually happy to contribute, but having the choice not to can help them with this. This is a crucial aspect of responding to children's individual needs and ensuring we focus on helping them to feel safe and secure before we expect them to change their behaviour. For example, a child who has been referred to the group because they find it hard to speak in class needs additional support, along with feeling safe, to develop the ability to do this.

Preparing for the group

In previous chapters I have discussed the importance of school staff using self-reflection as a tool to explore and monitor their own feelings. This is of particular value to the group facilitator and can be implemented by checking how they are feeling at the start and end of the session. It is good practice to have time to prepare the resources beforehand in a relaxed way, rather than rushing around looking for them at the last minute. I encourage the facilitator to spend a few minutes sitting in the room when it is prepared, before going to collect the children. Schools are extremely busy places and I appreciate how difficult this may be, but it is worth doing in order that the group is delivered in the most effective way possible. I suggest looking through the facilitator's guidelines (Chapters 11 and 12) and having them and the session plan accessible, so they can be referred to easily. The children are usually too involved in the activities to look at them, but the facilitator can acknowledge this by saying, 'These notes are to help me run our group well and I want to look at them to make sure I do it properly so we all have an enjoyable time.' If a facilitator forgets something or makes a mistake, then this should be acknowledged to the group. I once forgot to put their session charts out and I acknowledged it by saying I had forgotten and acknowledging that 'even adults forget things and make mistakes sometimes'. It is important that, as adults, we are able to model this for children, as it gives permission for them to admit to their mistakes more easily.

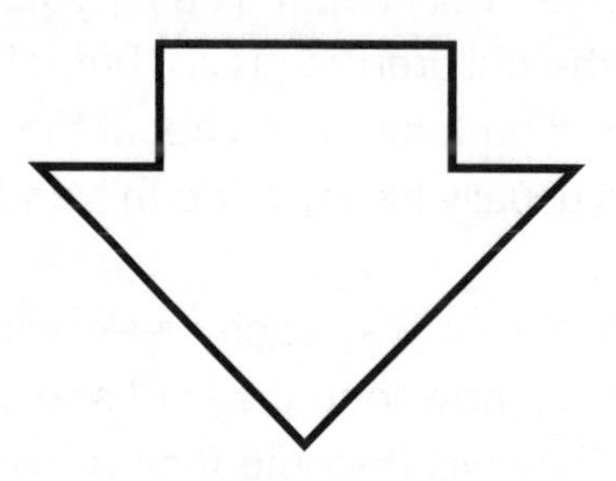

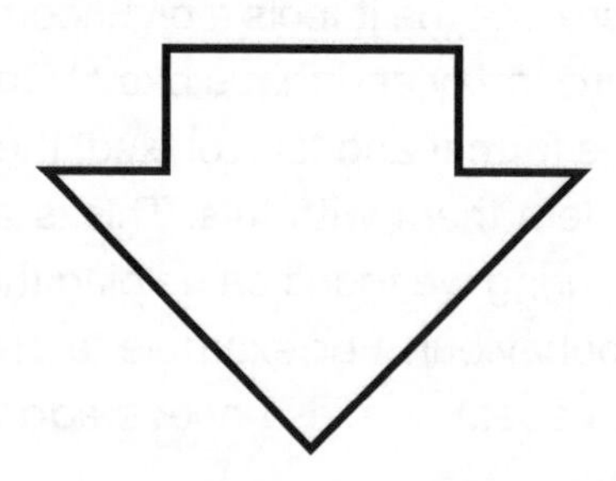

Figure 9.1 Potential negative impact of facilitator

The facilitator's use of their own internal check can be useful to develop self-awareness and appreciation of the importance of the tone of voice, body language and facial expressions being used. All of these will be communicating powerful messages to the children and are worth exploring and reflecting on afterwards. This can be useful to look at after the session when writing up the session notes. For example, if a session was particularly challenging, first explore how you felt: were you hungry, tired and a bit distracted thinking about what you had to do after the session? As the group work is a focused programme with a small group of children, it can be intense and tiring. In order for it to run most effectively, the facilitator should enjoy delivering the programme and look forward to its weekly occurrence, rather than dreading it.

organised and enthusiastic

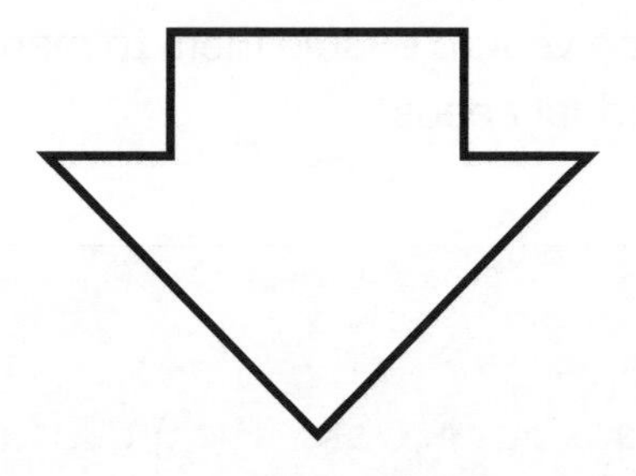

Child feels:

safe and relaxed

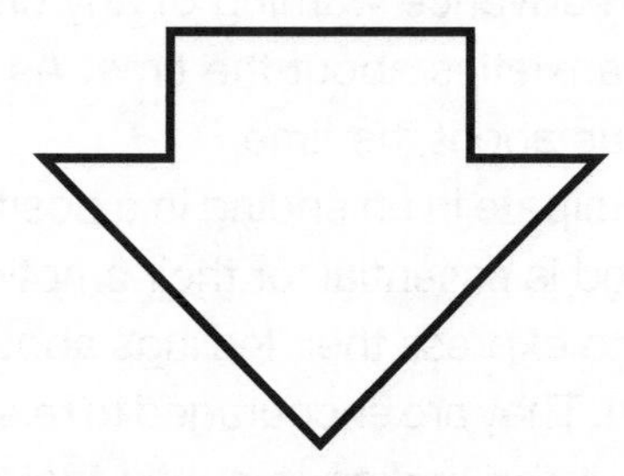

Group is:

productive and enjoyable

Figure 9.2 Potential positive impact of facilitator

The importance of endings

In the last session, it is essential that the ending is acknowledged. For some children the group work opportunity has been the highlight of their week so it is important that the loss of the weekly sessions is given the appropriate validation. There may be children in the group who have experienced many changes and losses in their lives, and these may not have been managed well, so it provides an opportunity for the group facilitator to provide them with a more positive experience. The ending of the group can be a good opportunity to validate the children's feelings about this and to be honest with them in a way that recognises and helps them manage their feelings.

The facilitator will start each session by stating the session number as the children are colouring in their session charts, and acknowledge the remaining number of sessions. For example, 'It's our fourth session today, so we have got two more sessions and then the sixth session will be our last one.' This provides the children with an opportunity to voice their feelings each week and provides the facilitator with an insight into how each child manages endings. This information can be shared with the children's existing teacher to help them assist the child to manage changes that may occur in class and at the end of the school year. It can also be passed on to the child's new class teachers at the start of each year to enable them to manage the transition to their class in a way that meets the child's individual needs.

Case study

Billy, aged 4, was very quiet and anxious in class. The group facilitator noticed that he was frequently looking at the clock during group sessions, especially when she mentioned the time.

The group facilitator was able to acknowledge this and provide him with reassurance that it was her job to remember the time so he didn't have to. She was also able to talk to his class teacher to ensure that Billy was given advance warning of any changes wherever possible, and to encourage her to be aware of his anxieties about the time. As the sessions progressed, Billy became more relaxed and less anxious about the time.

The opportunity for children to participate in an ending in a positive way and have their feelings about this acknowledged and validated is essential for their emotional well-being. During the last session, the facilitator is encouraged to express their feelings about the ending and acknowledge that this may be difficult for the children. They are encouraged to respond positively to the children's expression of their own feelings about the ending in a way that validates and 'contains' them. This positive event may provide the children with a completely different ending compared with others they have had previously, where people may just disappear overnight with no explanation being offered to them. This experience of endings provides them with a new template that is crucial for their emotional health.

10 'What ifs' for group work

The following reactions to events are rare and may never happen, but it is useful to be prepared for any responses you may experience:

- If a child doesn't want to come to a session, check with the child whether there is a reason. Reflect, 'It may feel a bit strange coming out of class,' and encourage them to come by saying, 'You can come and see what we are doing this week.'
- If a child comes to the session but is reluctant to join in, reflect, 'Maybe you are unsure about joining in today; you can just watch and see what we are going to do and join in when you feel like it.'
- If a child keeps looking at the clock, reflect, 'I can see you looking at the clock; maybe you are worried about the time because I put the stickers on to show the time, but I can check the time so you don't need to.'
- If there are disruptions to the session by meetings taking place in the room or drums playing loudly nearby, ensure all staff are made aware beforehand that the room will be in use. Acknowledge any noise outside and reflect, 'It can be difficult to concentrate when there is a lot of noise outside.'
- If people walk in during the session, remind them you are doing the group and ask them to come back later, put a sign on the door (see Resources section) and reflect, 'It's important that we're not disturbed because our time together is important.'
- If a child wants to take what they've made with them that week, reflect, 'You really want to take that with you today, but you can take everything with you on the last week.'
- If a child shares something about themselves; for example, 'I've not got a dad, I've just got a mum', listen to the child and respond appropriately. If the child needs to talk more, offer to have some time with them outside the group where they can talk to you. Ensure you pass on any concerns to the relevant member of staff in school.

11 Friendship programme and facilitator's guidelines

This chapter contains a weekly overview and facilitator's guidelines for each session. The weekly overview provides a summary of each week's session and activities. The facilitator's guidelines are more detailed and provide examples of reflections to use during the sessions. The group facilitator needs to take the facilitator's guidelines with them to each session.

The resources are in the Resources section at the end of the book.

Overview: week one

Beginning (3 minutes)

- Introduce the group and explain about the time and number of sessions.
- Encourage each child to sit on the floor, colour their chart and write their name on their folder.
- Explain that the group will start and end in the same way each week, but the activity in the middle will be different.
- Encourage them to put their session chart in their folder and explain you will look after them until the next session.

Middle (14 minutes)

- Explain that this week's activity is to decorate their folder.
- Show them the selection of materials available to use and give each child a glue stick.
- Encourage them to decorate their folder using the materials and pens.
- Explain that they can decorate them however they like; there is no right or wrong way.
- Explain that you will look after their folder and that you will keep everything until the last session when they can take it with them if they want to.

Ending (3 minutes)

- Explain that each session will end in the same way each week.
- Set the facial expression cards out on the floor and name the feeling on each face.
- Ask each child to point to or name the face that shows how they feel now.
- Explain that they can say why they feel like this if they want to, but they don't have to.
- Praise them for their hard work in the session and tell them you will see them at the same time and in the same room next week.
- Walk them back to their class.

Facilitator's guide: week one

Beginning (3 minutes)

- Ask the children to sit on the floor by their folders.
- Reflect, 'It may feel strange coming out of class (or nursery) with me today.'
- Reflect, 'It may feel uncomfortable at first as we don't know each other very well yet, but we will spend the next six weeks getting to know each other better.'
- Discuss that the group is a way of helping them to practise things such as sharing, taking turns and being good friends, and the activities will help them with this.
- Reflect, 'It's really important that you feel happy being in here and sharing your ideas. Some children find this easy and other children find it difficult, and that's because we are all different. It's okay in here if you need help with this.'
- If a child is looking round the room then reflect, 'I can see you are looking round the room; maybe it feels a bit strange coming in here.'
- Explain that you will see them every week for six weeks and if you need to miss a week due to a school trip or you or them not being at school, then they will have the session the following week so they will not miss it.
- Tell them you will see them at the same time on the same day each week and show them on the clock the start and end time. For example, 'When the big hand gets to the "6", we will go back to class.'
- Give each child a folder and a session chart.
- Encourage them to colour in week one on their chart and say they can choose which colour to use.
- Ask them to put the chart in their folder when they have finished.
- If a child needs help with this, reflect, 'It can be difficult to do this and I wonder if you would like some help with it.'
- Explain that they can write their name however they want to on their folder as it is theirs: 'You can do it in big or small writing, wherever you want to, as it's your folder.'
- If a child looks unsure, reflect, 'It seems as if you're not sure where or how to write it, but remember you can choose and there's no right or wrong way.'

Middle (14 minutes)

- Explain that this week's activity is to decorate their folder.
- Show them the selection of materials available to use and give each child a glue stick.
- Explain that they can use any of the materials they would like to.
- Explain that they can decorate them however they like and acknowledge, 'There is no right or wrong way to decorate them; they are your folders so you can decorate them however you want to.'
- Acknowledge, 'Your folders will probably look very different, and that's because you are different people and may not like the same things, and that's okay.'
- Explain that they are going to practise sharing the materials and waiting for the things they want to use; for example, 'Michael might want to use the blue pen that Jonah is using, so Michael could practise waiting for the pen and use something else instead until Jonah has finished with it.'
- Reflect, 'It can be hard to wait for things sometimes, but we can practise that in here.'

- If you notice a child looking at another child's folder or looking uncertain, reflect, 'It can be hard to decide what to do. I can see you looking at … (other child's) folder and maybe you think you should do the same, but remember we are all different and our folders will all be different too.'
- While they are decorating their folders, comment on what they are doing; for example, 'I can see you are both working hard to make your folders very special. I can see you are really thinking about what to use next.'
- Try and spend time focusing equally on each child's folder, but don't offer praise or positive comments yet, as this may influence what the other child does on their folder.
- While they are using the materials, acknowledge and praise any sharing of materials that occurs; for example, 'That was really kind of you to pass Holly the pot of stars, Sarah. It's nice to do kind things for other people.'
- If a child is finding it difficult to share or is holding on to one of the pots of materials, acknowledge this and reflect, 'I can see you holding on to the pot of shapes, Billy. It can be hard to share sometimes, but I wonder if you would be able to let James use them now.'
- If the child refuses or continues to hold the pot, reflect, 'I can see that's really difficult for you to do; perhaps you are worried there won't be enough for you; maybe you can take some out for you to use and give the pot to Billy.'
- Acknowledge the child's attempts to do this by reflecting, 'I can see that was very hard for you, so well done for sharing; that's very kind of you.'
- Acknowledge the time and let them know when they have a few minutes left. Reflect, 'It can be hard to stop when we are enjoying doing something, but we need to finish decorating our folders soon.'
- Acknowledge when they have one more minute and reflect, 'It's nearly time for us to stop decorating our folders, so just finish the last bit and then we will stop.'
- If a child continues after you have asked them to stop, reflect, 'I can see it's really hard for you to hear what I am saying and to stop, but that's what we need to do now.'
- Move the folders away from them and explain that you will look after them for them until the next session.

Ending (3 minutes)

- Explain that each session will end in the same way each week and reflect, 'It can help us if we know what we are going to do each week.'
- Set the facial expression cards out on the floor and encourage them to look at each one and name the feeling on each face. For example, 'I wonder how that person feels. Let's see if we can guess by looking at their face.'
- Explain that they are going to practise being able to say how they feel, and acknowledge, 'It's important that we try and say how we feel and then people can help us with those feelings, so if we feel sad and we tell someone, then they can help us to feel better.'
- Explain that at the end of each week you will ask them how they feel and encourage each child to point to or name the face that shows how they feel now.
- Explain that they can say why they feel like this if they want to, but they don't have to.
- Reflect, 'Sometimes it can be hard to know how we feel, but we can practise doing this in here.'
- Acknowledge, 'Everyone has lots of different feelings and sometimes we may feel happy or sad or cross or scared, and that's okay. Everyone feels like that sometimes.'
- Give examples of when people may have those feelings; for example, 'Sometimes we may feel scared when we are doing something for the first time. Maybe you both felt a bit scared when we were coming in here today because you didn't know what we would be doing.'

- If a child looks unsure or worried, reflect, 'It can be really hard to know how we feel. I am wondering if you feel happy or sad or cross or scared; maybe it would help if I pointed to each one and you can think about whether you feel like that.'
- When each child points or says how they feel, reflect it back to them by saying, 'You feel happy, Alfie. Thank you for telling us how you feel.'
- Praise them for their hard work in the session and tell them you will see them at the same time and in the same room next week.
- Walk them back to their class.

Overview: week two

Beginning (2 minutes)

- Encourage each child to sit on the floor by their folder and colour their chart.
- Explain that the group will start and end in the same way each week, but the activity in the middle will be different.
- Encourage them to put their session chart in their folder and explain you will look after them until the next session.

Middle (15 minutes)

- Explain that today you are going to draw a picture of each other and talk about being a good friend.
- Encourage each child to draw the other child and give the picture to the other child when they have finished.
- Give each child their folder to put the picture they have been given in.
- Explain that you will look after their folders and they can take them with them on the last week.

Ending (3 minutes)

- Explain that each session will end in the same way each week.
- Set the facial expression cards out on the floor and name the feeling on each face.
- Ask each child to point to or name the face that shows how they feel now.
- Explain that they can say why they feel like this if they want to, but they don't have to.
- Praise them for their hard work in the session and tell them you will see them at the same time and in the same room next week.
- Walk them back to their class.

Facilitator's guide: week two

Beginning (2 minutes)

- Ask the children to sit on the floor by their folders and session chart.
- Reflect, 'It may feel strange coming out of class (or nursery) with me today, as we don't know each other very well yet, but we will spend the next few weeks getting to know each other better.'
- Remind them that the group is a way of helping them to practise things such as sharing, taking turns and being good friends, and the activities will provide ways to help them with this.
- Reflect, 'It's really important that you feel happy being in here and sharing your ideas. Some children find this easy and other children find it difficult, and that's because we are all different. It's okay in here if you need help with this.'

- If a child is looking round the room then reflect, 'I can see you are looking round the room; maybe it feels a bit strange coming in here.'
- Remind them that you will see them every week and if you need to miss a week due to a school trip or you or them not being at school, then they will have the session the following week so they will not miss the session.
- Show them on the clock the start and end times. For example, 'When the big hand gets to the "6", we will go back to class.'
- Encourage them to colour in week two on their chart and say they can choose which colour to use.
- Ask them to put the chart in their folder when they have finished.
- If a child needs help with this, reflect, 'It can be difficult to do this and I wonder if you would like some help with it.'

Middle (15 minutes)

- Explain that this week they are going to make something for each other.
- Explain that today you are going to draw a picture of each other and talk about being friends.
- Give each child a piece of paper and encourage them to share the pens.
- Remind them they are practising sharing, taking turns and waiting in here.
- Acknowledge it's not always easy to do this, and remind them you will help them with this.
- Encourage each child to draw the other child and help them to think about and look at the other child. For example, 'It can help us to look at the other person when we are drawing them so we can see what they look like. You can look at each other's eyes or clothes and think about how you want to draw them and what colours you want to use.'
- If a child is looking unsure or hesitating to get started, reflect, 'Sometimes it can be difficult to start drawing a picture; maybe you can look at the pens and choose a colour you would like to use.'
- Spend equal time focusing on and acknowledging each child's pictures. For example, 'I can see you are looking closely at Lucy's jumper; maybe you are thinking about how to draw it.'
- While they are drawing their pictures, talk about being a friend and what friends might do, such as play with us, talk to us, listen to us, share things with us, etc.
- Acknowledge the time and let them know when they have a few minutes left. Reflect, 'It can be hard to stop when we are enjoying doing something, but we need to finish drawing our pictures soon.'
- Acknowledge when they have one more minute and reflect, 'It's nearly time for us to stop, so just finish drawing the last bit and then we will stop.'
- If a child continues after you have asked them to stop, reflect, 'I can see it's really hard for you to hear what I am saying and to stop, but that's what we need to do now.'
- Ask each child to give the picture they have drawn to the other child and ask each child to thank the other child for their picture.
- Praise both children for being able to do this; for example, 'Well done for being kind and drawing a picture for someone else.'
- If a child is reluctant to give their picture to the other child or says they want to keep it, reflect, 'It can be difficult to give something away when we have worked hard on it, but remember we are practising doing new things in here. It can be kind to do things for other people.'
- Ask each child to put the picture they have been given in their folder.
- Explain that you will look after their folders and they can take them with them on the last week.

Ending (3 minutes)

- Explain that each session will end in the same way each week and reflect, 'It can help us if we know what we are going to do each week.'
- Remind them that they are going to practise being able to say how they feel. Ask them how they feel and encourage each child to point to or name the face that shows how they feel now.
- Explain that they can say why they feel like this if they want to, but they don't have to.
- Reflect, 'Sometimes it can be hard to know how we feel, but we can practise doing this in here.'
- If a child looks unsure or worried, reflect, 'It can be really hard to know how we feel. I am wondering if you feel happy or sad or cross or scared; maybe it would help if I pointed to each one and you can think about whether you feel like that.'
- When each child points or says how they feel, reflect it back to them by saying, 'You feel sad, Alfie. Thank you for telling us how you feel.'
- Praise them for their hard work in the session and tell them you will see them at the same time and in the same room next week.
- Walk them back to their class.

Overview: week three

Beginning (2 minutes)

- Encourage each child to sit on the floor and colour their chart.
- Explain that the group will start and end in the same way each week, but the activity in the middle will be different.
- Encourage them to put their session chart in their folder and explain you will look after them until the next session.

Middle (15 minutes)

- Explain that this week you are going to talk about feelings a bit more.
- Give each child a feelings worm and go through each feeling one by one, asking them to draw a face to show each feeling under the word.
- Encourage each child to take turns pointing at the face and saying when they have felt like this. For example, 'I felt happy when it was my birthday.'
- Encourage each child to put the feelings worm in their folder and explain they can take it with them on the last week, if they want to.

Ending (3 minutes)

- Explain that each session will end in the same way each week.
- Set the facial expression cards out on the floor and name the feeling on each face.
- Ask each child to point to or name the face that shows how they feel now.
- Explain that they can say why they feel like this if they want to, but they don't have to.
- Praise them for their hard work in the session and tell them you will see them at the same time and in the same room next week.
- Walk them back to their class.

Facilitator's guide: week three

Beginning (2 minutes)

- Ask the children to sit on the floor by their folders and session chart.
- Reflect, 'We are getting to know each other a bit more now; maybe it feels easier coming out with me today.'
- Remind them that the group is a way of helping them to practise things such as sharing, taking turns and being good friends and the activities will provide ways to help them with this.
- Show them on the clock the start and end times. For example, 'When the big hand gets to the "6", we will go back to class.'
- Encourage them to colour in week three on their chart and say they can choose which colour to use.
- Ask them to put the chart in their folder when they have finished.
- If a child needs help with this reflect, 'It can be difficult to do this and I wonder if you would like some help with it.'

Middle (15 minutes)

- Explain that this week you are going to talk about feelings a bit more.
- Give each child a feelings worm and talk about each of the feelings one by one.
- Encourage them to think about and share examples of when people may experience the feelings, for example, 'When might people feel cross?'
- Encourage each child to share examples and reflect, 'Sometimes it can be hard to think about feeling sad or cross or scared.'
- If a child is reluctant to participate reflect, 'Some feelings are difficult to think about and talk about, but remember everyone feels sad, scared or cross sometimes.'
- Discuss each feeling one by one and ask them to draw a face to show each feeling under the word, for example, 'Draw a happy face under the word happy.'
- While they are drawing the faces talk about how having friends can help us with our feelings; for example, 'When we feel sad, playing with our friends might make us feel better.'
- Acknowledge the time and let them know when they have a few minutes left. Reflect, 'It can be hard to stop when we are enjoying doing something, but we need to finish drawing the faces soon.'
- Acknowledge when they have one more minute and reflect, 'It's nearly time for us to stop drawing the faces, so just finish the last bit and then we will stop.'
- When they have finished the faces, encourage each child to take turns pointing at the face and saying when they have felt like this; for example, 'I felt happy when it was my birthday.'
- If a child is unsure or can't think of an example, reflect, 'I can see you are unsure/don't want to talk and that's okay. It can be hard to share our feelings, but we can keep practising how to do it in here.'
- Encourage each child to put the feelings worm in their folder and remind them they can take it with them on the last week.
- Reflect, 'It can be hard when you've made something and want to take it with you today, but I'm going to keep all your things safe for you in your folder.'

Ending (3 minutes)

- Explain that each session will end in the same way each week and reflect, 'It can help us if we know what we are going to do each week.'

- Remind them that they are going to practise being able to say how they feel. Ask them how they feel and encourage each child to point to or name the face that shows how they feel now.
- Explain that they can say why they feel like this if they want to, but they don't have to.
- Reflect, 'Sometimes it can be hard to know how we feel, but we can practise doing this in here.'
- If a child looks unsure or worried, reflect, 'It can be really hard to know how we feel. I am wondering if you feel happy or sad or cross or scared; maybe it would help if I pointed to each one and you can think about whether you feel like that.'
- When each child points or says how they feel, reflect it back to them by saying, 'You feel sad, Alfie. Thank you for telling us how you feel.'
- Praise them for their hard work in the session and tell them you will see them at the same time and in the same room next week.
- Walk them back to their class.

Overview: week four

Beginning (2 minutes)

- Encourage each child to sit on the floor and colour their chart.
- Explain that the group will start and end in the same way each week, but the activity in the middle will be different.
- Encourage them to put their session chart in their folder and explain you will look after them until the next session.

Middle (15 minutes)

- Explain that this week they will be working together to make a model, and encourage them to think about what they would like to make.
- Give them a box of bricks and explain that they will be taking it in turns to choose a piece and put it on the model.
- When they have finished making it, explain that you will take a photo for them to put in their folder.

Ending (3 minutes)

- Explain that each session will end in the same way each week.
- Set the facial expression cards out on the floor and name the feeling on each face.
- Ask each child to point to or name the face that shows how they feel now.
- Explain that they can say why they feel like this if they want to, but they don't have to.
- Praise them for their hard work in the session and tell them you will see them at the same time and in the same room next week.
- Walk them back to their class.

Facilitator's guide: week four

Beginning (2 minutes)

- Ask the children to sit on the floor by their folders and session chart.
- Reflect, 'We are getting to know each other a bit more now; maybe it feels easier coming out with me today.'
- Remind them that the group is a way of helping them to practise things such as sharing, taking turns and being good friends, and the activities will provide ways to help them with this.

- Show them on the clock the start and end times. For example, 'When the big hand gets to the "6", we will go back to class.'
- Encourage them to colour in week four on their chart and say they can choose which colour to use.
- Ask them to put the chart in their folder when they have finished.
- If a child needs help with this, reflect, 'It can be difficult to do this and I wonder if you would like some help with it.'

Middle (15 minutes)

- Explain that this week they will be working together to make a model, and encourage them to think about what they would like to make and decide together.
- Acknowledge, 'It can be really difficult when one person wants to make something and the other person wants to make something else, but we can talk about this more and work out how we can agree on what to do.'
- If one child is being more vocal or monopolising the ideas, acknowledge this: 'I can hear you have lots of ideas, Marcus, and that's great, but let's see if Pria wants to share her ideas, too, because we are going to try and decide together what to make.'
- If they are finding it very hard to think of ideas, you can encourage them to think of things. For example, 'I am wondering if you would like to make a house or a boat or a plane.'
- Give them a box of bricks and explain that they will be taking it in turns to choose a piece and put it on the model.
- Reflect, 'It can be hard to wait your turn, but remember we are practising this in here and we can help each other to do this.'
- Encourage each child to take a piece and decide where they would like to put it on the model.
- If a child looks unsure or hesitant, reflect, 'I can see you looking at the model; maybe you are wondering where to put your piece.'
- Acknowledge the child who is waiting while the other child does this and reflect, 'It can be very hard to wait your turn and you are doing really well at waiting.'
- Acknowledge the time and let them know when they have a few minutes left. Reflect, 'It can be hard to stop when we are enjoying doing something, but we need to finish making our model soon.'
- Acknowledge when they have one more minute and reflect, 'It's nearly time for us to stop making the model, so you can have one more turn each and then we will stop.'
- When they have finished making it, praise them for working well together and explain that you will take a photo of it for them after the session and you will put in their folder.

Ending (3 minutes)

- Explain that each session will end in the same way each week and reflect, 'It can help us if we know what we are going to do each week.'
- Remind them that they are going to practise being able to say how they feel. Ask them how they feel and encourage each child to point to or name the face that shows how they feel now.
- Explain that they can say why they feel like this if they want to, but they don't have to.
- Reflect, 'Sometimes it can be hard to know how we feel, but we can practise doing this in here.'
- If a child looks unsure or worried, reflect, 'It can be really hard to know how we feel. I am wondering if you feel happy or sad or cross or scared; maybe it would help if I pointed to each one and you can think about whether you feel like that.'
- When each child points or says how they feel reflect it back to them by saying, 'You feel sad, Alfie. Thank you for telling us how you feel.'

- Praise them for their hard work in the session and tell them you will see them at the same time and in the same room next week.
- Walk them back to their class.

Overview: week five

Beginning (2 minutes)

- Encourage each child to sit on the floor and colour their chart.
- Explain that the group will start and end in the same way each week, but the activity in the middle will be different.
- Encourage them to put their session chart in their folder and explain you will look after them until the next session.

Middle (15 minutes)

- Explain that they will be decorating a butterfly for each other and give each child a butterfly.
- Explain that they can use the pens and collage materials to decorate them and make them nice for the other person.
- When they have finished them, ask each child to give their butterfly to the other child.
- Encourage each child to thank the child as they give them the butterfly.
- Ask each child to put their butterfly in their folder and explain that they can take it with them next week.

Ending (3 minutes)

- Explain that each session will end in the same way each week.
- Set the facial expression cards out on the floor and name the feeling on each face.
- Ask each child to point to or name the face that shows how they feel now.
- Explain that they can say why they feel like this if they want to, but they don't have to.
- Praise them for their hard work in the session and tell them you will see them at the same time and in the same room next week.
- Walk them back to their class.

Facilitator's guide: week five

Beginning (2 minutes)

- Ask the children to sit on the floor by their folders and session chart.
- Acknowledge it will be the last week next week and reflect, 'It may feel a bit sad to think about our group finishing.'
- Remind them that the group is a way of helping them to practise things such as sharing, taking turns and being good friends, and the activities will provide ways to help them with this.
- Show them on the clock the start and end time. For example, 'When the big hand gets to the "6", we will go back to class.'
- Encourage them to colour in week five on their chart and say they can choose which colour to use.
- Ask them to put the chart in their folder when they have finished.
- If a child needs help with this, reflect, 'It can be difficult to do this and I wonder if you would like some help with it.'

Middle (15 minutes)

- Explain that they will be decorating a butterfly for each other and give each child a butterfly.
- Acknowledge that this may be a difficult thing to do and reflect, 'Liam, it may feel hard to give your butterfly that you have made to Max, but it is a kind thing to do and we are practising doing kind things in here.'
- Explain that they can use the pens and collage materials to decorate them and make them nice for the other person.
- Explain that they can choose which things they would like to use and give each child a glue stick.
- If a child is unsure or hesitant, reflect, 'I can see you looking at all the things; maybe you are not sure what to use. Remember, you can use whatever you would like to.'
- If a child is looking at or starts to copy the other child, reflect, 'I can see you looking at ... (other child's name) butterfly and maybe you think you should do yours the same, but your butterfly will look different as you are both different people and may like using different things.'
- Ensure you spend equal time acknowledging each child's work and commenting on what they are doing (without praising them, as this may influence what the other child does). For example, 'I can see you are working very hard on colouring your butterfly.'
- If a child starts commenting or trying to control how the other child is decorating their butterfly, reflect, 'I can hear it's really hard for you to let ... (other child's name) decorate it how he wants to, and maybe you would like him to make it different for you, but it's important that he chooses how to make your butterfly special for you and that you choose how to decorate his butterfly that you are making for him.'
- Acknowledge the time and let them know when they have a few minutes left. Reflect, 'It can be hard to stop when we are enjoying doing something, but we need to finish making your butterfly soon.'
- Acknowledge when they have one more minute and reflect, 'It's nearly time for us to stop making your butterfly.'
- When they have finished them, ask each child to give their butterfly to the other child.
- If a child is reluctant or unsure, reflect, 'I know you worked really hard on your butterfly and maybe you wish that you could keep it for yourself, but remember we said we were making it for each other, so it would be very kind if you gave it to ... (other child's name).'
- Encourage each child to thank the other child as they give them the butterfly.
- Ask each child to put their butterfly in their folder and explain that they can take it with them next week.

Ending (3 minutes)

- Explain that each session will end in the same way each week and reflect, 'It can help us if we know what we are going to do each week.'
- Remind them that they are going to practise being able to say how they feel. Ask them how they feel and encourage each child to point to or name the face that shows how they feel now.
- Explain that they can say why they feel like this if they want to, but they don't have to.
- Reflect, 'Sometimes it can be hard to know how we feel, but we can practise doing this in here.'
- If a child looks unsure or worried, reflect, 'It can be really hard to know how we feel. I am wondering if you feel happy or sad or cross or scared; maybe it would help if I pointed to each one and you can think about whether you feel like that.'
- When each child points or says how they feel reflect it back to them by saying, 'You feel sad, Alfie. Thank you for telling us how you feel.'

- Praise them for their hard work in the session and tell them you will see them at the same time and in the same room next week.
- Walk them back to their class.

Overview: week six

Beginning (2 minutes)

- Encourage each child to sit on the floor and colour their chart.
- Encourage them to put their session chart in their folder and explain they can take it home with them today.

Middle (15 minutes)

- Explain that this week they are going to draw round each other's hand and give both children a worksheet.
- Ask each child to draw round the other child's hand on both worksheets.
- Ask each child to write their name in the box on their worksheet and the other child's worksheet.
- Ask each child to take the contents of their folder out and look at all the work they have done.
- Encourage them to put everything back in their folder to take home with them.

Ending (3 minutes)

- Give each child their folder and explain that they can take them with them if they would like to.
- Acknowledge the positive changes that have occurred, e.g. 'I remember when it was hard for you to wait your turn, but now you are both really good at it.'
- Acknowledge how hard they have all worked and how much you have enjoyed spending time with them.
- Walk them back to their class.

Facilitator's guide: week six

Beginning (2 minutes)

- Ask the children to sit on the floor by their folders and session chart.
- Show them on the clock the start and end time. For example, 'When the big hand gets to the "6", we will go back to class.'
- Encourage them to colour in week six on their session chart and say they can choose which colour to use.
- Ask them to put the chart in their folder when they have finished.
- If a child needs help with this, reflect, 'It can be difficult to do this and I wonder if you would like some help with it.'
- Remind them that this is their last week and respond appropriately to any comments they make. For example, 'I know it may feel sad as we've worked together for six weeks.'
- While they are doing this you can acknowledge any memorable moments for you. For example, 'I remember when you drew the pictures of each other and worked really hard to make them nice for each other.'

- Respond appropriately to any comments the children make about any memories they have by reflecting, 'I hear you've got some good memories of our time together in the group, too.'

Middle (15 minutes)

- Explain that this week they are going to draw round each other's hand and give both children a worksheet.
- Ask one child to put their hand on the worksheet and encourage the other child to draw round the other child's hand.
- Repeat this so there is a template of each child's hand on the worksheet.
- Repeat this on the other child's worksheet.
- Ask each child to write their name in the box on their worksheet and the other child's worksheet.
- Ask each child to take the contents of their folder out and look at all the work they have done.
- If there is time, they can colour their own worksheet.
- Encourage them to put everything back in their folder to take home with them.

Ending (3 minutes)

- Set the facial expression cards out on the floor and encourage each child to say how they feel.
- When each child points or says how they feel, reflect it back to them by saying, 'You feel sad, Alfie. Thank you for telling us how you feel.'
- Acknowledge that 'sometimes endings can feel sad. I have really enjoyed spending time with you both and you've both worked very hard in here. Although we won't have our group any more, we will still see each other around school, which I know won't be the same, but you can always come and talk to me if you want to.'
- Acknowledge the positive changes that have occurred, e.g. 'I remember when it was hard for you to wait your turn, but now you are both really good at it.'
- Acknowledge how hard they have all worked and how much you have enjoyed spending time with them.
- Give each child their folder and explain that they can take them with them if they would like to.
- Walk them back to their class.

12 Self-esteem programme and facilitator's guidelines

This chapter contains a weekly overview and facilitator's guidelines for each session. The weekly overview provides a summary of each week's session and activities. The facilitator's guidelines are more detailed and provide examples of reflections to use during the sessions. The group facilitator needs to take the facilitator's guidelines with them to each session.

The resources are in the Resources section at the end of the book.

Overview: week one

Beginning (3 minutes)

- Introduce the group and explain about the time and number of sessions.
- Encourage each child to sit on the floor, colour their chart and write their name on their folder.
- Explain that the group will start and end in the same way each week, but the activity in the middle will be different.
- Encourage them to put their session chart in their folder and explain you will look after them until the next session.

Middle (14 minutes)

- Explain that this week's activity is to decorate their folder.
- Show them the selection of materials available to use and give each child a glue stick.
- Encourage them to decorate their folder using the materials and pens.
- Explain that they can decorate them however they like; there is no right or wrong way.
- Explain that you will look after their folder and that you will keep everything until the last session when they can take it with them if they want to.

Ending (3 minutes)

- Explain that each session will end in the same way each week.
- Set the facial expression cards out on the floor and name the feeling on each face.
- Ask each child to point to or name the face that shows how they feel now.
- Explain that they can say why they feel like this if they want to, but they don't have to.
- Praise them for their hard work in the session and tell them you will see them at the same time and in the same room next week.
- Walk them back to their class.

Facilitator's guide: week one

Beginning (3 minutes)

- Ask the children to sit on the floor by their folders.
- Reflect, 'It may feel strange coming out of class (or nursery) with me today.'
- Reflect, 'It may feel uncomfortable at first as we don't know each other very well yet, but we will spend the next six weeks getting to know each other better.'
- Discuss that the group is a way of helping them to practise things such as sharing, taking turns and being good friends, and the activities will help them with this.
- Reflect, 'It's really important that you feel happy being in here and sharing your ideas. Some children find this easy and other children find it difficult, and that's because we are all different. It's okay in here if you need help with this.'
- If a child is looking round the room then reflect, 'I can see you are looking round the room; maybe it feels a bit strange coming in here.'
- Explain that you will see them every week for six weeks and if you need to miss a week due to a school trip or you or them not being at school, then they will have the session the following week so they will not miss it.
- Tell them you will see them at the same time on the same day each week and show them on the clock the start and end times. For example, 'When the big hand gets to the "6", we will go back to class.'
- Give each child a folder and a session chart.
- Encourage them to colour in week one on their chart and say they can choose which colour to use.
- Ask them to put the chart in their folder when they have finished.
- If a child needs help with this, reflect, 'It can be difficult to do this and I wonder if you would like some help with it.'
- Explain that they can write their name however they want to on their folder as it is theirs: 'You can do it in big or small writing, wherever you want to, as it's your folder.'
- If a child looks unsure reflect, 'It seems as if you're not sure where or how to write it, but remember you can choose and there's no right or wrong way.'

Middle (14 minutes)

- Explain that this week's activity is to decorate their folder.
- Show them the selection of materials available to use and give each child a glue stick.
- Explain that they can use any of the materials they would like to.
- Explain that they can decorate them however they like and acknowledge, 'There is no right or wrong way to decorate them; they are your folders so you can decorate them however you want to.'
- Acknowledge, 'Your folders will probably look very different, and that's because you are different people and may not like the same things and that's okay.'
- Explain that they are going to practise sharing the materials and waiting for the things they want to use; for example, 'Michael might want to use the blue pen that Jonah is using, so Michael could practise waiting for the pen and use something else instead until Jonah has finished with it.'
- Reflect, 'It can be hard to wait for things sometimes, but we can practise that in here.'
- If you notice a child looking at another child's folder or looking uncertain, reflect, 'It can be hard to decide what to do. I can see you looking at … (other child's) folder and maybe you think you should do the same, but remember we are all different and our folders will all be different too.'

- While they are decorating their folders, comment on what they are doing; for example, 'I can see you are both working hard to make your folders very special. I can see you are really thinking about what to use next.'
- Try and spend time focusing equally on each child's folder, but don't offer praise or positive comments yet, as this may influence what the other child does on their folder.
- While they are using the materials, acknowledge and praise any sharing of materials that occurs, for example, 'That was really kind of you to pass Holly the pot of stars, Sarah. It's nice to do kind things for other people.'
- If a child is finding it difficult to share or is holding on to one of the pots of materials acknowledge this and reflect, 'I can see you holding on to the pot of shapes, Billy. It can be hard to share sometimes, but I wonder if you would be able to let James use them now.'
- If the child refuses or continues to hold the pot, reflect, 'I can see that's really difficult for you to do; perhaps you are worried there won't be enough for you; maybe you can take some out for you to use and give the pot to Billy.'
- Acknowledge the child's attempts to do this by reflecting, 'I can see that was very hard for you so well done for sharing; that's very kind of you.'
- Acknowledge the time and let them know when they have a few minutes left. Reflect, 'It can be hard to stop when we are enjoying doing something, but we need to finish decorating our folders soon.'
- Acknowledge when they have one more minute and reflect, 'It's nearly time for us to stop decorating our folders, so just finish the last bit and then we will stop.'
- If a child continues after you have asked them to stop, reflect, 'I can see it's really hard for you to hear what I am saying and to stop, but that's what we need to do now.'
- Move the folders away from them and explain that you will look after them for them until the next session.

Ending (3 minutes)

- Explain that each session will end in the same way each week and reflect, 'It can help us if we know what we are going to do each week.'
- Set the facial expression cards out on the floor and encourage them to look at each one and name the feeling on each face. For example, 'I wonder how that person feels. Let's see if we can guess by looking at their face.'
- Explain that they are going to practise being able to say how they feel and acknowledge, 'It's important that we try and say how we feel and then people can help us with those feelings, so if we feel sad and we tell someone, then they can help us to feel better.'
- Explain that at the end of each week you will ask them how they feel and encourage each child to point to or name the face that shows how they feel now.
- Explain that they can say why they feel like this if they want to, but they don't have to.
- Reflect, 'Sometimes it can be hard to know how we feel, but we can practise doing this in here.'
- Acknowledge, 'Everyone has lots of different feelings and sometimes we may feel happy or sad or cross or scared, and that's okay. Everyone feels like that sometimes.'
- Give examples of when people may have those feelings, for example, 'Sometimes we may feel scared when we are doing something for the first time. Maybe you both felt a bit scared when we were coming in here today because you didn't know what we would be doing.'
- If a child looks unsure or worried, reflect, 'It can be really hard to know how we feel. I am wondering if you feel happy or sad or cross or scared; maybe it would help if I pointed to each one and you can think about whether you feel like that.'

- When each child points or says how they feel reflect it back to them by saying, 'You feel happy Alfie. Thank you for telling us how you feel.'
- Praise them for their hard work in the session and tell them you will see them at the same time and in the same room next week.
- Walk them back to their class.

Overview: week two

Beginning (2 minutes)

- Encourage each child to sit on the floor by their folder and colour their chart.
- Explain that the group will start and end in the same way each week, but the activity in the middle will be different.
- Encourage them to put their session chart in their folder and explain you will look after them until the next session.

Middle (15 minutes)

- Explain that this week they are going to make a feelings faces chart and give each child a chart.
- Explain what each word says and ask them to draw a face under each one to show the feeling.
- Discuss when people may feel like this as they are drawing each face.
- Give each child their folder to put the chart they have made in.
- Explain that you will look after their folders and they can take them with them on the last week.

Ending (3 minutes)

- Explain that each session will end in the same way each week.
- Set the facial expression cards out on the floor and name the feeling on each face.
- Ask each child to point to or name the face that shows how they feel now.
- Explain that they can say why they feel like this if they want to, but they don't have to.
- Praise them for their hard work in the session and tell them you will see them at the same time and in the same room next week.
- Walk them back to their class.

Facilitator's guide: week two

Beginning (2 minutes)

- Ask the children to sit on the floor by their folders and session chart.
- Reflect, 'It may feel strange coming out of class (or nursery) with me today, as we don't know each other very well yet, but we will spend the next few weeks getting to know each other better.'
- Remind them that the group is a way of helping them to practise things such as sharing, taking turns and being good friends, and the activities will provide ways to help them with this.
- Reflect, 'It's really important that you feel happy being in here and sharing your ideas, some children find this easy and other children find it difficult, and that's because we are all different. It's okay in here if you need help with this.'
- If a child is looking round the room, then reflect, 'I can see you are looking round the room; maybe it feels a bit strange coming in here.'

- Remind them that you will see them every week and if you need to miss a week due to a school trip or you or them not being at school, then they will have the session the following week so they will not miss the session.
- Show them on the clock the start and end times. For example, 'When the big hand gets to the "6", we will go back to class.'
- Encourage them to colour in week two on their chart and say they can choose which colour to use.
- Ask them to put the chart in their folder when they have finished.
- If a child needs help with this reflect 'It can be difficult to do this and I wonder if you would like some help with it.'

Middle (15 minutes)

- Explain that this week they are going to make a feelings faces chart and give each child a chart.
- Explain what each word says one at a time and share examples of when people may have those feelings. For example, 'This word says "cross": it can make us feel cross if we are playing with something and another child tries to take it away from us. I wonder if you can think of a time when you have felt cross.'
- Ask each child to draw a face under each word to show the feeling. For example, 'We have been talking about what makes us feel cross: can you draw a cross face under the word that says "cross"?'
- If a child is unsure or reluctant to give an example, reflect, 'It can be hard to think about and talk about how we feel sometimes. If you do not want to talk about how you feel, that's okay.'
- Go through each of the words one by one and talk about the feeling. Give them an example and encourage them to share examples of when they have felt like this.
- Respond positively to each child's contribution and acknowledge their feelings; for example, 'Thank you for telling us you felt scared when your mum shouted, Tom. It can be scary when someone shouts.'
- Monitor the time and ensure there is enough time to discuss each feeling and draw each facial expression.
- Acknowledge when they have one more minute and reflect, 'It's nearly time for us to stop, so just finish drawing the last bit and then we will stop.'
- Acknowledge and praise them for sharing their feelings. For example, 'Well done for talking about your feelings today; sometimes that can be a difficult thing to do.'
- Give each child their folder to put the chart they have made in.
- Explain that you will look after their folders and they can take them with them on the last week.

Ending (3 minutes)

- Explain that each session will end in the same way each week and reflect, 'It can help us if we know what we are going to do each week.'
- Remind them that they are going to practise being able to say how they feel. Ask them how they feel and encourage each child to point to or name the face that shows how they feel now.
- Explain that they can say why they feel like this if they want to, but they don't have to.
- Reflect, 'Sometimes it can be hard to know how we feel, but we can practise doing this in here.'
- If a child looks unsure or worried, reflect, 'It can be really hard to know how we feel. I am wondering if you feel happy or sad or cross or scared; maybe it would help if I pointed to each one and you can think about whether you feel like that.'

- When each child points or says how they feel, reflect it back to them by saying, 'You feel sad, Alfie. Thank you for telling us how you feel.'
- Praise them for their hard work in the session and tell them you will see them at the same time and in the same room next week.
- Walk them back to their class.

Overview: week three

Beginning (2 minutes)

- Encourage each child to sit on the floor and colour their chart.
- Explain that the group will start and end in the same way each week, but the activity in the middle will be different.
- Encourage them to put their session chart in their folder and explain you will look after them until the next session.

Middle (15 minutes)

- Explain that this week they are going to take turns looking at objects and then feeling them without looking and trying to guess what they are.
- Look at and encourage them to take turns feeling and naming the objects before putting them in the bag.
- Encourage them to take turns putting their hand in the bag and describing the object and guessing what it is.

Ending (3 minutes)

- Explain that each session will end in the same way each week.
- Set the facial expression cards out on the floor and name the feeling on each face.
- Ask each child to point to or name the face that shows how they feel now.
- Explain that they can say why they feel like this if they want to, but they don't have to.
- Praise them for their hard work in the session and tell them you will see them at the same time and in the same room next week.
- Walk them back to their class.

Facilitator's guide: week three

Beginning (2 minutes)

- Ask the children to sit on the floor by their folders and session chart.
- Reflect, 'We are getting to know each other a bit more now; maybe it feels easier coming out with me today.'
- Remind them that the group is a way of helping them to practise things such as sharing, taking turns and being good friends and the activities will provide ways to help them with this.
- Show them on the clock the start and end times. For example, 'When the big hand gets to the "6", we will go back to class.'
- Encourage them to colour in week three on their chart and say they can choose which colour to use.
- Ask them to put the chart in their folder when they have finished.
- If a child needs help with this reflect, 'It can be difficult to do this and I wonder if you would like some help with it.'

Middle (15 minutes)

- Explain that this week they are going to take turns looking at objects and then feeling them without looking and trying to say how they feel and guess what they are.
- Look at and encourage them to take turns naming the objects and feeling them before putting them in the bag; for example, 'I wonder what this is and I wonder how it feels.'
- Encourage them to take turns putting their hand in the bag and describing the object and guessing what it is before taking the object out.
- Reflect, 'It can be hard to wait for your turn; you are doing really well at waiting to have your turn.'
- If a child starts taking the object out before naming it, encourage them to stop and try and guess what it is.
- Acknowledge the time and let them know when they have a few minutes left. Reflect, 'It's nearly time for us to stop doing this activity, so you can just have one more turn each and then we will stop.'
- Praise them for their hard work in the session and tell them you will see them at the same time and in the same room next week.
- Walk them back to their class.

Ending (3 minutes)

- Explain that each session will end in the same way each week and reflect, 'It can help us if we know what we are going to do each week.'
- Remind them that they are going to practise being able to say how they feel. Ask them how they feel and encourage each child to point to or name the face that shows how they feel now.
- Explain that they can say why they feel like this if they want to, but they don't have to.
- Reflect, 'Sometimes it can be hard to know how we feel, but we can practise doing this in here.'
- If a child looks unsure or worried, reflect, 'It can be really hard to know how we feel. I am wondering if you feel happy or sad or cross or scared; maybe it would help if I pointed to each one and you can think about whether you feel like that.'
- When each child points or says how they feel reflect it back to them by saying, 'You feel sad, Alfie. Thank you for telling us how you feel.'
- Praise them for their hard work in the session and tell them you will see them at the same time and in the same room next week.
- Walk them back to their class.

Overview: week four

Beginning (2 minutes)

- Encourage each child to sit on the floor and colour their chart.
- Explain that the group will start and end in the same way each week, but the activity in the middle will be different.
- Encourage them to put their session chart in their folder and explain you will look after them until the next session.

Middle (15 minutes)

- Explain that this week they will be decorating a heart for each other and give both children a heart template.

- Encourage them to decorate it using the felt pens and materials provided and discuss how it can feel to make something for someone else.
- When they have finished, encourage each child to give the heart to the other child and give them their folder to put it in.
- Explain that you will look after their folders and they can take them with them on the last week.

Ending (3 minutes)

- Explain that each session will end in the same way each week.
- Set the facial expression cards out on the floor and name the feeling on each face.
- Ask each child to point to or name the face that shows how they feel now.
- Explain that they can say why they feel like this if they want to, but they don't have to.
- Praise them for their hard work in the session and tell them you will see them at the same time and in the same room next week.
- Walk them back to their class.

Facilitator's guide: week four

Beginning (2 minutes)

- Ask the children to sit on the floor by their folders and session chart.
- Reflect, 'We are getting to know each other a bit more now; maybe it feels easier coming out with me today.'
- Remind them that the group is a way of helping them to practise things such as sharing, taking turns and being good friends, and the activities will provide ways to help them with this.
- Show them on the clock the start and end times. For example, 'When the big hand gets to the "6", we will go back to class.'
- Encourage them to colour in week four on their chart and say they can choose which colour to use.
- Ask them to put the chart in their folder when they have finished.
- If a child needs help with this, reflect, 'It can be difficult to do this and I wonder if you would like some help with it.'

Middle (15 minutes)

- Explain that this week they are going to make something for each other.
- Give each child a heart template and a glue stick and explain that they are going to decorate it and make it special for the other person.
- Encourage them to decorate it using the felt pens and materials provided and remind them that they are practising sharing and taking turns in here.
- Acknowledge, 'It can sometimes be difficult to share things, but we are practising doing that in here to help you both get much better at it. It helps to practise doing things.'
- If a child is looking unsure or hesitating to get started, reflect, 'Sometimes it can be difficult to start making something; maybe you are unsure what to do. Remember, you can choose how you would like to decorate it.'
- While they are decorating the hearts, discuss how it can feel to make something for someone else.
- Acknowledge, 'It is kind to make things for other people; it can make us feel happy when someone makes something for us.'

- Spend equal time focusing on and acknowledging each child's heart. For example, 'I can see you are working hard to make that special.'
- If a child starts commenting or trying to control how the other child is decorating their heart, reflect, 'I can hear it's really hard for you to let … (other child's name) decorate it how he wants to, and maybe you would like him to make it different for you, but it's important that he chooses how to make your heart special for you and that you choose how to decorate his heart that you are making for him.'
- Acknowledge the time and let them know when they have a few minutes left. Reflect, 'It can be hard to stop when we are enjoying doing something, but we need to finish making the hearts soon.'
- Acknowledge when they have one more minute and reflect, 'It's nearly time for us to stop, so just finish doing the last bit and then we will stop.'
- If a child continues after you have asked them to stop, reflect, 'I can see it's really hard for you to hear what I am saying and to stop, but that's what we need to do now.'
- Ask each child to give the heart they have decorated to the other child and ask each child to thank the other child for their picture.
- Praise both children for being able to do this; for example, 'Well done for being kind and making something for someone else.'
- If a child is reluctant to give their heart to the other child or says they want to keep it, reflect, 'It can be difficult to give something away when we have worked hard on it, but remember we are practising doing new things in here. It can be kind to do things for other people.'
- Ask each child to put the heart they have been given in their folder.
- Explain that you will look after their folders and they can take them with them on the last week.

Ending (3 minutes)

- Explain that each session will end in the same way each week and reflect, 'It can help us if we know what we are going to do each week.'
- Remind them that they are going to practise being able to say how they feel. Ask them how they feel and encourage each child to point to or name the face that shows how they feel now.
- Explain that they can say why they feel like this if they want to, but they don't have to.
- Reflect, 'Sometimes it can be hard to know how we feel, but we can practise doing this in here.'
- If a child looks unsure or worried, reflect, 'It can be really hard to know how we feel. I am wondering if you feel happy or sad or cross or scared; maybe it would help if I pointed to each one and you can think about whether you feel like that.'
- When each child points or says how they feel reflect it back to them by saying, 'You feel sad, Alfie. Thank you for telling us how you feel.'
- Praise them for their hard work in the session and tell them you will see them at the same time and in the same room next week.
- Walk them back to their class.

Overview: week five

Beginning (2 minutes)

- Encourage each child to sit on the floor and colour their chart.
- Explain that the group will start and end in the same way each week, but the activity in the middle will be different.
- Encourage them to put their session chart in their folder and explain you will look after them until the next session.

Middle (15 minutes)

- Explain that they will be decorating their name and give each child a piece of card with their name on it.
- Explain that they can use the pens to decorate them and make them nice for themselves.
- Ask each child to put their name card in their folder and explain that they can take it with them next week.

Ending (3 minutes)

- Explain that each session will end in the same way each week.
- Set the facial expression cards out on the floor and name the feeling on each face.
- Ask each child to point to or name the face that shows how they feel now.
- Explain that they can say why they feel like this if they want to, but they don't have to.
- Praise them for their hard work in the session and tell them you will see them at the same time and in the same room next week.
- Walk them back to their class.

Facilitator's guide: week five

Beginning (2 minutes)

- Ask the children to sit on the carpet by their folders and session chart.
- Acknowledge it will be the last week next week and reflect, 'It may feel a bit sad to think about our group finishing.'
- Show them on the clock the start and end times. For example, 'When the big hand gets to the "6", we will go back to class.'
- Encourage them to colour in week five on their chart and say they can choose which colour to use.
- Ask them to put the chart in their folder when they have finished.
- If a child needs help with this reflect, 'It can be difficult to do this and I wonder if you would like some help with it.'

Middle (15 minutes)

- Explain that they will be decorating their name and give each child a piece of card with their name on it and a glue stick.
- Explain that they can use the pens to decorate them and make them nice for themselves.
- Acknowledge, 'Last week you made something special for each other and this week you are making something special for yourselves. It can feel nice to make something special for ourselves.'
- Encourage them to decorate it using the felt pens and remind them that they are practising sharing and taking turns in here.
- Acknowledge, 'It can sometimes be difficult to share things, but we are practising doing that in here to help you both get much better at it, and I can see that you are both getting really good at it.'
- If a child is looking unsure or hesitating to get started, reflect, 'Sometimes it can be difficult to start making something; maybe you are unsure what to do. Remember, you can choose how you would like to decorate it.'
- While they are decorating their name cards, spend equal time focusing on and acknowledging each child's work. For example, 'I can see you are working hard to make that special.'

- Acknowledge the time and let them know when they have a few minutes left. Reflect, 'It can be difficult to stop when we are enjoying doing something, but you need to finish decorating your names soon.'
- Acknowledge when they have one more minute and reflect, 'It's nearly time for us to stop, so just finish doing the last bit and then we will stop.'
- If a child continues after you have asked them to stop, reflect, 'I can see it's really hard for you to hear what I am saying and to stop, but that's what we need to do now.'
- Ask each child to put their name card in their folder and explain that they can take it with them next week.

Ending (3 minutes)

- Explain that each session will end in the same way each week and reflect, 'It can help us if we know what we are going to do each week.'
- Remind them that they are going to practise being able to say how they feel. Ask them how they feel and encourage each child to point to or name the face that shows how they feel now.
- Explain that they can say why they feel like this if they want to, but they don't have to.
- Reflect, 'Sometimes it can be hard to know how we feel, but we can practise doing this in here.'
- If a child looks unsure or worried, reflect, 'It can be really hard to know how we feel. I am wondering if you feel happy or sad or cross or scared; maybe it would help if I pointed to each one and you can think about whether you feel like that.'
- When each child points or says how they feel reflect it back to them by saying, 'You feel sad, Alfie. Thank you for telling us how you feel.'
- Praise them for their hard work in the session and tell them you will see them at the same time and in the same room next week.
- Walk them back to their class.

Overview: week six

Beginning (2 minutes)

- Encourage each child to sit on the floor and colour their chart.
- Encourage them to put their session chart in their folder and explain they can take it home with them today.

Middle (15 minutes)

- Explain that this week they are going to make their own 'I am proud of me' medal and give each child a medal.
- Encourage them to decorate it and talk about being proud and what that means.
- Ask each child to take the contents of their folder out and look at all the work they have done.
- Encourage them to put everything back in their folder to take home with them.

Ending (3 minutes)

- Give each child their folder and explain that they can take them with them, if they would like to.
- Acknowledge the positive changes that have occurred, e.g. 'I remember when it was hard for you to wait your turn, but now you are both really good at it.'
- Acknowledge how hard they have all worked and how much you have enjoyed spending time with them.
- Walk them back to their class.

Facilitator's guide: week six

Beginning (2 minutes)

- Ask the children to sit on the floor by their folders and session chart.
- Show them on the clock the start and end times. For example, 'When the big hand gets to the "6", we will go back to class.'
- Encourage them to colour in week six on their session chart and say they can choose which colour to use.
- Ask them to put the chart in their folder when they have finished.
- If a child needs help with this reflect, 'It can be difficult to do this and I wonder if you would like some help with it.'
- Remind them that this is their last week and respond appropriately to any comments they make, e.g. 'I know it may feel sad as we've worked together for six weeks.'
- While they are doing this you can acknowledge any memorable moments for you, e.g. 'I remember when you decorated the hearts for each other and worked really hard to make them nice for each other.'
- Respond appropriately to any comments the children make about any memories they have by reflecting, 'I hear you've got some good memories of our time together in the group, too.'

Middle (15 minutes)

- Explain that this week they are going to make their own 'I am proud of me' medal and give each child a medal.
- Offer them a selection of pens to decorate one side of the medal.
- Remind them about sharing the pens and acknowledge, 'You have been working really hard at practising sharing and taking turns in here each week, so let's see if we can practise sharing again with the pens.'
- Encourage them to decorate the medal and talk about being proud and what that means. For example, 'We may feel proud when we have done something well or we have tried hard at doing something; we can feel proud when we have been kind or someone praises us.'
- Encourage each child to think about and share when they have done something they feel proud of. For example, 'I wonder if we can think about when we have felt proud of ourselves.'
- If a child is unsure or hesitant, reflect, 'It can be hard to think of when we have been proud of ourselves; I wonder if you can think about something you have done well or been pleased about.'
- If a child is still finding it difficult to think of something they are proud of then you can share something you have seen them do in the group. For example, 'I remember when you made the heart for ... (other child's name) and you worked really hard to make it special. I was proud of how hard you worked on it.'
- On the back of the medal write what the child says they are proud of; for example, 'I am proud of me because I am a good friend.'
- Acknowledge the time and let them know when they have a few minutes left. Reflect, 'It can be hard to stop when we are enjoying doing something, but you need to finish doing your medals soon.'
- Acknowledge when they have one more minute and reflect, 'It's nearly time for us to stop, so just finish doing the last bit and then we will stop.'
- If a child continues after you have asked them to stop, reflect, 'I can see it's really hard for you to hear what I am saying and to stop, but that's what we need to do now.'

- Put the ribbon on the medal and ask each child if they would like to wear the medal or put it in their folder.
- Ask each child to take the contents of their folder out and look at all the work they have done.
- Encourage them to put everything back in their folder to take home with them.

Ending (3 minutes)

- Set the facial expression cards out on the floor and encourage each child to say how they feel.
- When each child points or says how they feel reflect it back to them by saying, 'You feel sad, Alfie. Thank you for telling us how you feel.'
- Acknowledge that 'sometimes endings can feel sad. I have really enjoyed spending time with you both and you've both worked very hard in here. Although we won't have our group any more, we will still see each other around school, which I know won't be the same, but you can always come and talk to me if you want to.'
- Acknowledge the positive changes that have occurred, e.g. 'I remember when it was hard for you to wait your turn, but now you are both really good at it.'
- Acknowledge how hard they have all worked and how much you have enjoyed spending time with them.
- Give each child their folder and explain that they can take them with them if they would like to.
- Walk them back to their class.

Conclusion

The impact that good educational practice can have on children and families is invaluable. I hope I have demonstrated that schools have a crucial role to play in developing positive mental health and well-being in children, in turn preventing further difficulties in adult life and problems for society as a whole. Our prisons and mental health systems have a large percentage of adults who had difficult early experiences as children that they have carried into their adult lives. We have a responsibility as a society to break the perpetuation of that cycle by providing opportunities for the next generation of young people to have experiences that promote positive mental health and emotional well-being.

There are endless possibilities throughout the school day to introduce emotional vocabulary, provide children with skills and opportunities to express their feelings, and produce experiences that enable them to learn about their emotional health and well-being. Schools are in an ideal position to provide children with positive and nurturing relationship experiences that can offer children an alternative relational template to the one they may have within their family. When we meet children's emotional and social needs, we remove the barriers that create blockages and enable them to learn.

The group work programme is an ideal opportunity to do this in a way that can be easily integrated into the school day with minimal disruption and maximum success. It enables schools to do things differently and provide children with opportunities to experience new ways of understanding and managing their feelings. As adults, we may try to protect children from experiencing sadness, hurt and upset, but these are part of life, along with happiness, joy and excitement. Our task as practitioners is to support children with understanding and experiencing all feelings, not just some feelings. Children have a strong foundation for later life if they can manage their own feelings, understand the feelings of others and interact positively with other people.

Every child deserves to be happy, safe and settled in school and to be equipped with the skills to build friendships, the confidence to do well and the opportunity to reach their full potential. Children need the opportunity to feel they belong, are worthwhile, have something to offer and can make a contribution to the world. Children need to feel they have a purpose in the same way as adults do.

We've got to get it right for children from now. There are generations of children who have had negative experiences of school, resulting in negative views of themselves and taking those experiences into adulthood, therefore increasing the likelihood of ending up in our prisons or mental health systems, having children of their own and repeating the cycle. The long-term consequences for individuals, families and society as a whole of children being emotionally unhealthy and having poor relational skills are enormous. We need to take children's mental health seriously. If we invest in children's emotional health and well-being, we provide them with potential skills for life. If we don't, we provide them with potential problems for life.

Resources

This section contains all the resources needed to prepare, plan and evaluate the group work programmes. These can be photocopied and prepared in advance of the programme. The resources include:

- a register
- session notes to be completed at the end of each session
- guidelines for completing intervention questionnaires
- start and end of intervention questionnaires
- a completed example of a group work report
- a blank format of a group work report
- a door sign.

Resources for delivering friendship group:

- overall resources list
- child session chart to be completed each week
- bookmark template
- butterfly template
- kind hands words
- scenarios
- medal template

Resources for delivering self-esteem:

- overall resources list
- child session chart to be completed each week
- balloon template
- heart template
- kind words for balloon
- star template
- 'My favourite' worksheet
- story and questions

Group work questionnaires guidelines for group facilitators

- Ask the child's class teacher or teaching assistant to complete the start questionnaires for each child that will be in the group with you.
- Ensure they complete each question and include additional comments about the child and how they are generally in class, at break times and around school. For example, Kevin can be quiet and withdrawn at times, or, Mia finds it hard to wait her turn and is frequently fighting with other children at lunchtime.
- Ask the same person to complete the end questionnaire for each child, ensuring they complete the section about any other changes that have occurred. For example, Kevin is more confident and is sharing his ideas more in class, or, Mia is being more patient and is gradually developing more friendships with the other children in the class.
- Compare each question using the start and end questionnaire for each child.
- Identify any positive changes that have occurred in the scoring; for example, a child who could only sometimes take turns but is now able to more frequently, along with any comments from the person who completed the end questionnaire.
- List the positive changes and write a paragraph describing how you experienced the child in the group sessions; for example, at first Jamie found it difficult to follow the group rules and kept interrupting while the other children were talking. However, after several gentle reminders and support from the group he was able to do this more easily. He became more confident at sharing his feelings and was able to acknowledge that he felt sad that the group was finishing.

Group work start of intervention questionnaire

Child's name:
Date of birth:

Please complete the following questions based on your knowledge of the child during the last month:

	Yes	No	Sometimes
Is this child able to share?			
Is this child able to make friends easily?			
Is this child kind to other children?			
Is this child able to take turns?			
Does this child have friends?			
Is this child popular?			
Does this child have conflicts with other children?			
Does this child bully other children?			
Does this child do what adults ask?			
Does this child offer to help?			
Does this child tell lies?			
Does this child find it difficult to concentrate?			
Does this child focus and engage with their learning?			
Does this child fidget and appear restless?			
Does this child appear to be anxious, worried or scared?			
Does this child have angry outbursts or tantrums?			
Is this child able to express their feelings easily?			
Does this child appear to be confident?			
Does this child say they feel unwell?			
Does this child appear to be happy?			

Any other comments:

Signed:
Date:

Group work report

Child's name:	Jane Jordan
Date of birth:	12.10.2011
Type of group:	Friendship
Group facilitator:	Nathan Crompton
Group dates:	June–July 2015
Questionnaire evaluation:	The questionnaires show that Jane has made several positive changes since being in the group. She is able to share more easily with gentle reminders and lots of praise. Her concentration has improved and she is less restless and fidgety.
Staff comments:	Her class teacher is very pleased with the progress Jane has made and has noticed that her friendships have improved. She feels she is more confident now and seems to be happier in herself.
Facilitator's comments:	Jane was very fidgety and anxious at the start of the group work sessions. She found it very hard to share the resources and initially kept taking things from the other child. However, with lots of praise and encouragement she gradually began sharing with the other child and started to initiate this herself as the sessions progressed.
Recommendations:	Jane may still need support with sharing and lots of praise and encouragement when she achieves this.
Signed:	
Date:	

Group work report

Child's name:
Date of birth:
Type of group:
Group facilitator:
Group dates:
Questionnaire evaluation:
Staff comments:
Facilitator's comments:
Recommendations:
Signed:
Date:

Group work in progress

Please do not disturb

Group work register

Please record the date that each group work session takes place and tick whether or not the child attended.

Name of child	Date	Date	Date	Date	Date	Date

Signed ....

Print name ....

Date ....

Group work session notes

Group work facilitator ....

Type of group ....

Date	Session number	Session detail and comments (it is useful to make notes on individual children and group dynamics)

Resources for friendship group

- clock
- mat or rug for the floor
- register and session record (to be completed each week)
- folder for both children (the same colour)
- weekly chart for both children
- felt pens
- facial expression cards
- collage materials (weeks one and five)
- glue stick for both children (weeks one and five)
- plain A4 paper (week two)
- feelings worm (week three)
- bricks (week four)
- camera or iPad (week four)
- butterfly template (week five)
- worksheet (week six)
- pencil for both children (week six)

1
2
3
4
5
6

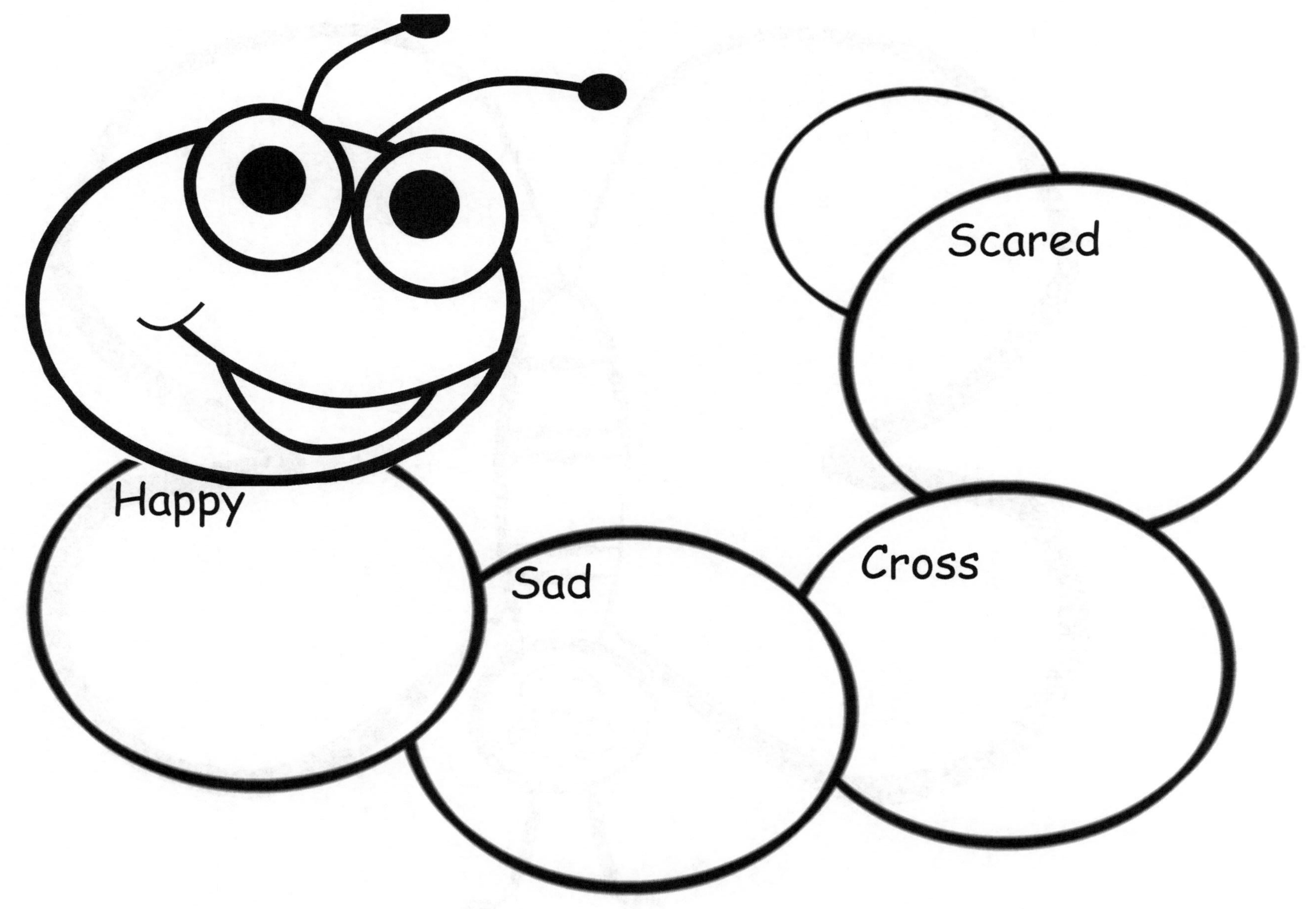

Happy
Sad
Cross
Scared

My hand	My friend's hand

SCARED

SAD

CROSS

HAPPY

Resources for self-esteem group

- clock
- mat or rug for the floor
- register and session record (to be completed each week)
- folder for both children (the same colour)
- weekly chart for both children
- felt-tip pens
- facial expression cards (please refer back to the facial expression cards in the friendship section)
- glue sticks for both children (weeks one, two and four)
- collage materials (weeks one and four)
- feelings faces chart (week two)
- feely bag and six objects, e.g. tissue, teddy, ball, etc. (week three)
- heart template (week four)
- name card (week five)
- medal (week six)
- ribbon (week six)
- hole punch (week six)

6
1
2
3
4
5

HAPPY	SAD
CROSS	SCARED

I am proud of me...

Index

Page numbers in *italics* denote figures, those in **bold** denote tables.

absences, staff 46
achievement awards 9
activities *see* friendship activities; self-esteem activities
adults: significant 73–5; unpredictable 9, 10, 14, 20, 35, 57, **59**, 70; *see also* parents; staff
affirmative language 51, 86
anxiety 21; children's coping strategies 19, 31, 35, 36–7, 39–40, 58; learning to manage 3–6, 22–3, 58–9; physical signs of 34, **34**; staff responses to 68–9
appearance 10–11
approachability 68
assessments 9, 44, 61
assumptions 44
attendance officers 24
attention seeking 14, 21, 23, 32
attentiveness *see* vigilance, constant
awards, achievement 9

behaviour, children's: cycle of misunderstanding 35–7, *36*, *38*; impacts of adult responses on 49, 65, **65**; impacts of group work on 79–80, **80**; responding to 32–3, 71–2; understanding 29–42, **30**, **37**; *see also* behavioural expectations; coping strategies
behaviour, parenting *see* parenting behaviour
behaviour, staff 49, 65, **65**
behavioural expectations 5, 12, 54–5; community/school differences 27–8; focusing on 72–3; home/school differences 14–15, 19–21, **20**, 36; using affirmative language 51; visual reminders 5, 44
behaviour charts 55
behaviour system, school 54; *see also* behavioural expectations
belief systems, internal 19, **19**, 25, **25**, 31, 59–60, **59**
belonging, sense of 62, 80–1
benefits of group work 79–87
blaming: others 12, 14; self 19, 31, 59–60
body language 68, 95
bullying 10, 32, **37**, 40, 53, 63–4
butterfly decorating activity 107, 108, 136

changes: last group work session 96; moving classes 46–7, 96; moving schools 27, 64; multiple transitions 64; in school day 46; staff absences 46; staff leaving 68
chaotic families 34
child protection concerns 90
choices, learning to make 7, 9–10, 52, 81, 86
class teachers: managing absences of 46; sharing information with 89, 96; *see also* staff
codes of behaviour *see* behavioural expectations
cognitive understanding 33, 44, 61
communication: adult/child differences 29–30; developing skills 85; difficulties with 41; non-verbal 33, 68, 95
community/school differences 27–8
composition of group 91–2
confidence 6, 7, 8–10, 11, 69, 85–6
conflicting messages: community/school 27–8; home/school 14–15, 19–21, **20**, 36, 59–60
consequences, learning about 12, 52, 81
consistency: group work sessions 15, 81, 92; of staff 45, 46; *see also* inconsistent parenting

contradictions *see* conflicting messages
controlling behaviour 10, 14, 18, 20, 40
coping strategies 36–7; of children who feel unsafe 39–40; constant vigilance 14, 19, 39, 68, 92; controlling behaviour 10, 14, 18, 20, 40; disinterest 34; internal dialogues 31; overconfidence 10; rituals 35; self-reliance 7–8, 57, 68; soothing objects 30, 35, 58–9
core beliefs *see* internal belief systems
corporal punishment 21
courage 13
critical parenting 11, 14, 19, 25
cycle of misunderstanding 35–7, *36*, *38*

danger, alertness for 14, 39
decisions, learning to make 7, 9–10, 52, 81, 86
delayed gratification 3–4
development, staff 83–4
developmental levels 9, 14, 19, 35, 44
dialogues, internal 31
disappointment 13, 45
disengaged children 34, **37**, 40
domestic violence 10, 26–7, 49, 58, **59**
door sign 92, 130
drama, need to create 14, 23

embarrassment 53
emotional health 3–16; impacts of group work on 15–16, **15**; impacts of parenting behaviour on 9, 11, 14–15; and inconsistencies 8, 14; independence 6–7, 8; links with physical well-being 34, **34**; overconfidence 10; personal responsibility 11–12; resilience 13, 45, 81; self-awareness 11–12, 81; self-belief 11; self-confidence 8–10; self-esteem 6, 8–10, 25, 69; self-image 10–11; self-regulation 3–6, 11, 22–3; self-reliance 6, 7–8, 57, 68
'emotionally absent' parents 15, 25, 57, 59
emotional safety 53–4
emotional vocabulary 5, 9, 13, 33–4, 50, 51–2
emotions *see* feelings
empathy 61
endings: last group work session 96; staff leaving 68
English as a second language 41
excitement: difficulty tolerating 41; need to create 14, 23
expectations *see* behavioural expectations
external circumstances 17–28; community/school differences 27–8; domestic violence 10, 26–7, 49, 58, **59**; home/school differences 14–15, 19–21, **20**, 36, 59–60; moving schools 27, 64; parental attitudes to school 23–4; pressures on parents 25–6, 35, 58; *see also* families; parenting behaviour; parents

facial expression cards 83, **83**, 98, 100–1, 111, 113, 138–41
facial expressions 34, 68, 95
facilitators *see* group facilitators
families: chaotic 34; domestic violence 10, 26–7, 49, 58, **59**; expressing feelings 23, **23**; home/school differences 14–15, 19–21, **20**, 36, 59–60; relational experiences within 24–5, 57–8, 59–61, **59**, **61**; stress within 25–6, 35, 58; *see also* parenting behaviour; parents
family workers 7, 24
fear: children's coping strategies 19, 31, 35, 39–40, 58; of feelings 4, 9; learning to face 13; living in constant 14, 26, 27; of new experiences 9, 22; physical signs of 34, **34**; staff responses to 68–9
feelings: expressing through behaviour 30, **30**; expressing within families 23, **23**; fear of 4, 9; impact of school day on 43, **43**; learning to manage 3–6, 12, 13, 22–3, **23**, 41–2, 45; physical signs of 34, **34**; releasing 6; of staff 50; suppressing 31, 39; validation of 15, 33–4, 43, 82–3, **83**
feelings boards 34
feelings faces activity 114, 115, 144
feelings worm activity 103, 104, 135
feely bag activity 85, 88, 116, 117
fighting 41
folders for group work 93, 98, 99–100, 111, 112–13
format of group work sessions 92–3
friendship activities: butterfly decorating 107, 108, 136; feelings worm 103, 104, 135; folder decorating 98, 99–100; hand drawing 109, 110, 137; model making 105, 106; picture drawing 101, 102
friendship programme 98–110; resources 125, 133–41; week one 98–101; week two 101–3; week three 103–5; week four 105–7; week five 107–9; week six 109–10
friendships 61–3
frustration management 13

gender pressures 27
group facilitators: developing new skills 83–4; preparing for group sessions 93–5, *94*, *95*; role of 6, 88–90; self-reflection 93, 95
group work: benefits of 79–87; children who may benefit from 85–6, 91–2; development of relationships 62, 83; impacts on behaviour 79–80, **80**; impacts on emotional health 15–16, **15**; staff development 83–4; validation of feelings 15, 82–3, **83**; within whole school approach 55–6
group work questionnaires 88, 126, 127
group work register 92, 131
group work reports 90, 128, 129
group work sessions 91–6; composition of group 91–2; consistency 15, 81, 92; format 92–3; impacts of facilitators on 93–5, *94*, *95*; last session 96; rules 93; time keeping 81, 83, 92, 93; 'what ifs' 97; *see also* friendship programme; self-esteem programme

hand drawing activity 109, 110, 137
heart decorating activity 117–19, 145
help, ability to ask for 7–8, 68, 86
holidays, school 20, 46–7
home/school differences 14–15, 19–21, **20**, 36, 59–60
honesty 12
hyper vigilance 14, 19, 39, 68, 92

'I am proud of me' medals 121, 122–3, 146
impulse control 3–4
inconsistent parenting 8, 14, 20, 57, **59**
independence 6–7, 8
information sharing 89, 96
instructions, difficulty in retaining 40
internal belief systems 19, **19**, 25, **25**, 31, 59–60, **59**
internal dialogues 31
interrupting **20**, 51, 69

kind hands chart 63
kindness, understanding concept 12, 63

lateness 53
life skills 55–6
listening to children 51
lunchtime organisers 45
lunchtimes 45
lying 21–2

manipulative behaviour 10, 14, 18, 20, 40
medal making activity 121, 122–3, 146
mental health teams 90
mistakes, making 11–12, 21–2, 54, 69, 94
misunderstanding, cycle of 35–7, *36*, *38*
model making activity 105, 106
morale, staff 48
motivational vocabulary 11
moving classes 46–7, 96
moving schools 27, 64
multiple transitions 64
mute, selective 41

name cards activity 120–1
needs, recognition of 17–19
new experiences, fear of 9, 22
non-verbal communication 33, 68, 95
'notice me ' behaviours 14; *see also* attention seeking

objects: feely bag activity 85, 88, 116, 117; soothing 30, 35, 58–9
outside agencies 90
overconfidence 10
overprotective parenting 6–7, 14
ownership, sense of 35, 52, 80–1

parenting behaviour: critical 11, 14, 19, 25; impacts of 9, 11, 14–15, 17–19, **18**, **19**; inconsistent 8, 14, 20, 57, **59**; overprotective 6–7, 14; underprotective 14; unpredictable 9, 10, 14, 20, 35, 57, **59**, 70
parents: attitudes to school 23–4; 'emotionally absent' 15, 25, 57, 59; expressing feelings 23, **23**; external pressures on 25–6, 35, 58; involving in school 55; relationships with children 24–5, 57–8, 59–61, **59**, **61**; separating from 6, 30; sharing information with 89; supporting 7; *see also* families

patience 12, 85
perseverance 82
personal responsibility 11–12; *see also* responsibility
physical environment: group work sessions 92; school 52
physical well-being 17, **17**, 34, **34**
picture drawing activity 101, 102
positive messages 38–9, 50–1, **50**, 74–5, 84, *84*
predictability: group work sessions 15, 81, 92; of staff 46; *see also* unpredictable adults

questionnaires 88, 126, 127
quiet children 79–80, **80**, 85–6

reflection: use in group work 89, *89*; *see also* self-reflection, staff
reflective language 38–9, 50–1, **50**, 84, *84*
register, group work 92, 131
relational expectations, home/school differences 59–60
relational templates 60–1, **61**, 63, 68
relationships 57–70; bullying 10, 32, **37**, 40, 53, 63–4; difficulties building 57, 62–3, 67; early experiences of 57–9; friendships 61–3; impacts of group work on 62, 83; parents and children 24–5, 57–8, 59–61, **59**, **61**; sibling 61; between staff 47, 48, 69–70; staff and children 47, 48, 64–9, 73–5; staff leaving 68
reminders, visual 5, 44
reports, group work 90, 128, 129
resilience 13, 45, 81
resources 125–46; butterfly template 136; door sign 130; facial expression cards 138–41; feelings faces chart 144; feelings worm template 135; friendship programme 125, 133–41; group work register 131; group work reports 128, 129; hand drawing chart 137; heart template 145; 'I am proud of me' medal template 146; questionnaires 126, 127; self-esteem programme 125, 142–6; session charts 134, 143; session notes 132
responsibility: being given too much or too little 14; developing personal 11–12; opportunities to take 44, 52
rituals 35
rules: group work sessions 93; *see also* behavioural expectations
running away 41

sabotaging situations 31, 41, 91
safety: awareness of 52–3; emotional 53–4; feeling unsafe 39–40
school behaviour system 54; *see also* behavioural expectations
school day 44–5; emotional impact of 43, **43**; lunchtimes 45; managing changes in 46; visual plan of 46
school environment 43–4; awareness of safety 52–3; emotional safety 53–4; involving parents 55; making happier 75; physical 52; useful attributes **54**; *see also* school day; staff
school holidays 20, 46–7
school rules *see* behavioural expectations
security, sense of 10, 19, 57
selective mute 41
self, sense of 6, 8, 12, 13, 14, 18, 25
self-awareness: children 11–12, 81; staff 43, 95
self-belief 11
self-confidence 8–10
self-control 11, 81
self-esteem 6, 8–10, 25, 69
self-esteem activities: feelings faces charts 114, 115, 144; feely bags 85, 88, 116, 117; folder decorating 111, 112–13; heart decorating 117–19, 145; 'I am proud of me' medals 121, 122–3, 146; name cards 120–1
self-esteem programme 111–23; resources 125, 142–6; week one 111–14; week two 114–16; week three 116–17; week four 117–19; week five 119–21; week six 121–3
self-image 10–11
self-reflection, staff 47, 49, 64, 93, 95
self-regulation 3–6, 11, 22–3
self-reliance 6, 7–8, 57, 68
self-worth 8, 11, 14, 18, 25, **25**
SENCOs (special educational needs coordinators) 90
sense of self 6, 8, 12, 13, 14, 18, 25
separation issues: from parents 6, 30; staff absences 46
session charts 93, 98, 99, 111, 112, 134, 143
session notes 88, 92–3, 95, 132
sessions, group work *see* group work sessions
shame 14, 21, 53, 54
sharing 62
shouting 4, 46, 49, **65**

sibling relationships 61
significant adults 73–5
sitting quietly 32
skills: communication 85; developing new 7, 82; life 55–6; social 44, 61–3, 85
social and emotional developmental levels 9, 14, 19, 35, 44, 61
social skills 44, 61–3, 85
speaking: choosing not to 41; communication skills 85; quiet children 79–80, **80**
special educational needs coordinators (SENCOs) 90
staff: absences 46; appropriate behaviour 49, 65, **65**; developing new skills 83–4; leaving 68; lunchtime organisers 45; managing own feelings 50; morale 48; mutual support 49, 65; own experiences of school 65–6; qualities needed 47–8; relationships between 47, 48, 69–70; relationships with children 47, 48, 64–9, 73–5; self-reflection 47, 49, 64, 93, 95; as significant adults 73–5; support workers 67; training 48; *see also* group facilitators
stress management: children 3–6, 22–3; staff 65
stress within families 25–6, 35, 58
supply teachers 46
support workers 67
swearing **20**, 21

talking *see* speaking
tantrums 4, **20**, 33
targets for children 55
teachers: managing absences of 46; sharing information with 89, 96; supply 46; *see also* staff
time keeping in group sessions 81, 83, 92, 93
timetable, visual 46
tone of voice 68, 95
training, staff 48
transitions: multiple 64; to new classes 46–7, 96; to new schools 27, 64
traumatic experiences 10; *see also* domestic violence
trust 9–10, 44, 93

underprotective parenting 14
unpredictable adults 9, 10, 14, 20, 35, 57, **59**, 70
unsafe, feeling 39–40; *see also* fear

vigilance, constant 14, 19, 39, 68, 92
violence, domestic 10, 26–7, 49, 58, **59**
visual plan of school day 46
visual reminders 5, 44
vocabulary: emotional 5, 9, 13, 33–4, 50, 51–2; motivational 11; opportunities to expand 86
voice, tone of 68, 95

waiting 32, 85
well-being: physical 17, **17**, 34, **34**; *see also* emotional health
'what ifs' 97
whole school approach 43–4, 55–6